Holiday
Ideas

BARBOUR
PUBLISHING, INC.
Uhrichsville, OH

© MCMXCVII by Barbour Publishing, Inc.

ISBN 1-55748-962-9

Published by: Barbour Publishing, Inc.
P.O. Box 719
Uhrichsville, OH 44683
http://www.barbourbooks.com

Member of the
Evangelical Christian
Publishers Association

Printed in the United States of America.

Traditions to Make

THANKFUL HANDS

O n Thanksgiving we put a paper-cut handprint, in the form of a praying hand, on each plate set at the dinner table. Each handprint has the name of one of our guests on it. We put this name face down. During Thanksgiving dinner we take turns telling why we are thankful for the person whose name appears on our handprint.

A GINGERBREAD STABLE

Because my husband is German we make gingerbread houses at Christmastime. However, last year we made a gingerbread stable, baby Jesus, Mary, Joseph, and the animals instead. I think the children enjoyed making this one even more. My husband's German heritage as well as our Christian heritage were celebrated at once.

Julie Grunwald resides in Tucson, Arizona.

A HUMBLE TREE

My husband and I live in a small trailer. We tried using artificial trees and live cedar and pine trees for Christmas trees, but had problems with them for various reasons (cost and pine needles, cedar prickles stuck in our carpet, to name a few). We decided to start our own tradition, our "Charlie Brown" Christmas tree. We cut the top off a maple or similar tree, the kind with no leaves. We take small white tree lights and wrap them around the branches from top to bottom. We have also created theme Christmas trees by using just bows, or just glass ornaments. With no greenery on the tree, the white twinkling lights really make the tree decorations stand out. Also, by just cutting the top off the tree, the tree continues to live.

Jean C. Summey resides in Rock Hill, South Carolina.

IT'S A WRAP!

Make your own wrapping paper. Rubber stamping on brown packing paper, plain white wrapping paper, or even brown paper grocery bags can be an economical way to wrap your gifts. It is a lot of fun to design your own paper and it makes your gifts seem more personal. Children also love to design and stamp their own paper. Matching gift cards are easily made by folding an index card in half. Rubber stamps can also be used to make your own Christmas cards, or just to brighten up the envelopes of your store-bought cards!

Linda Slaughter resides in Park Ridge, Illinois.

A LASTING LEGACY

Perhaps you have grandchildren who receive far too many material items at Christmas. Why not purchase a savings bond, or silver coins that could have some value for them in the future! Coin packets, purchased for each year of their life, could be one legacy you leave for them.

Joyce Friesner resides in Ligonier, Indiana.

CHRISTMAS PUPPETS

Our children are at the ages now when they love to put on puppet shows. Shortly before Christmas we tell them the Christmas story in installments and they then make puppets of the characters that were in the story that day. (Any type of puppet will do.) We do this until the story and all the puppets have been completed. Then on Christmas Eve they put on their own performance, from the angel visiting Mary to the family fleeing to Egypt. (Painting or coloring scenery is optional but it adds a lot to the show!)

Christine Beckett resides in Matawan, New Jersey.

VERSATILE BASKETS

Gift baskets make great gifts. You can make your own baskets or buy plain ones and decorate them with ribbons and lace. Place fabric, a towel, or a doily inside as a lining. Customize the basket according to the receiver's personality, likes and dislikes, and so on. Here are some ideas: fishing tackle, soaps, perfumes, cards and travel games, CDs or cassettes, jewelry, miniatures or collectables, books, stationery, candy, jam, bathtub toys, doll clothes, tools, sewing things, socks, and so on. Be creative!

Loretta Arts resides in Valdez, Alaska.

CHRISTMAS MEMORY ALBUM

Our family's Christmas memories have been put together in a family Christmas album. Inside are photographs, descriptions of our celebrations, current world events, and many thoughts of the holiday. I look forward to the day when my children are grown and they too can treasure the album.

Annette McEndarfer resides in
Worcester, Massachusetts.

SCENTED TREE ORNAMENTS

Last year my sister and I invited my mother and her four sisters to my house to make these ornaments. It was a wonderful reason to get together and have lunch and "just talk."

1 cup applesauce	3/4 cup cinnamon
2 T. ground cloves	2 T. nutmeg
2 T. ginger	

Mix all ingredients together. Roll onto wax paper until 1/8-inch thick. Cut out with cookie cutters. Poke hole with a drinking straw to hang. Put on wire rack and dry three days, turning daily.

Since they have to dry in one place friends and relatives have another reason to "have to get together again" to claim the ornaments.

P.S. Another good idea might be to make these ornaments on Thanksgiving and use them as favors when you get together again for Christmas.

Linda J. Beck resides in Chicora, Pennsylvania.

HERB SHAKERS

One shake enlivens salads, meat, poultry, and vegetables!
To make, mix together the following herbs:

2 tsp. garlic powder   2 tsp. onion powder
2 tsp. paprika   2 tsp. white pepper
2 tsp. dry mustard   1 tsp. powdered thyme
1 tsp. ground celery seed

I buy antique salt shakers at garage sales or flea markets
and fill with herb shaker recipe to give as gifts.
June Blackford resides in Nicholasville, Kentucky.

A CHILD'S VERY OWN TREE

You will need a little pine tree or branch about four or
five inches tall, a plant pot, some dirt, popcorn, and anything else you wish for decorations.

Take the pot and fill it with dirt and plant the tree in
the pot. Take the popcorn and put it on the pine needles.
Then put it in your room. You will have your very own
Christmas tree!
Alicia Del Vescova resides in Round Top, New York.

A WREATH TO PASS ON

I became a single father when my daughter was three and
my son was one. Changing houses, starting day care, and
trying to rebuild a new life was a challenge to tradition and
routine. Christmas found us in the habit of reading a Bible

chapter every night during our snack, right before bed. I decided to introduce the Advent wreath tradition into our readings, making sure that we started and finished the Christmas story between Thanksgiving and December 25th.

After picking out our reusable wreath, I placed the manger figures of Mary, Joseph, and Jesus in the center, snuggled into Colorado evergreens. Then, I put the crèche with the animal figures toward the bottom and into the greenery of the Christmas tree, about child-eye level.

We know when Christmas has arrived because Old St. Nick not only finishes his cookies and milk, he also places Mary, Joseph, and the baby Jesus into the crèche, announcing the birth and highlighting the real meaning of Christmas.

Through the years we have collected a series of angels to hover around the créche, making it an eye catcher to all who see the tree. By Christmas Eve, my now ten- and thirteen-year old children have found the ornaments that look like tiny wrapped packages and have placed those near the base of the crèche as presents for the new baby. I look forward, as a grandpa someday, to seeing this tradition repeated in two other homes.

Patrick, John, and Lauren Batchelder reside in
Boulder, Colorado.

IN REMEMBRANCE

At Christmas we especially think of loved ones no longer with us. To remember, with joy instead of sadness, is sometimes difficult. I chose to make a remembrance ornament for my son Monte using a picture of him sitting at a Christmas tree that was a happy memory. It is meaningful to me, a small remembrance, made with great love. The spirit of Christmas is giving with love, and remembering with love.

Frances Moss Taylor resides in Danville, Virginia.

KEEP WINTER BRIGHT

After Christmas is over, I put the greeting cards I received in an attractive basket next to the phone and use them for notes. Each time I make a note I reread and enjoy the holiday message once again and remember happy times with the friend or relative who sent the card to me. One of the best things about Christmas is being in touch with dear ones. In this way, Christmas brightens all the winter months.

*Mary Louise Colln is a writer of
inspirational romance and
also works as a registered nurse.
She resides in Joplin, Missouri.*

CHRISTMAS CARDS PLUS

Each fall we have our family picture taken at a place that offers mini-portrait packages. We then enclose in Christmas cards our picture, a newsletter (a summary of the past year written by each family member), and a Gospel tract. It is a good opportunity to show God's love toward others and to witness of His presence in our lives during the past year.

GIFTS FOR GRANDMOTHERS

For years I faced the dilemma of what to give my grandmothers for Christmas. They did not need or want ornamental objects or "things." So I tried something different a few years ago: I put together a decorated box filled with delightful items. Small cans of fruits or vegetables, puddings, crackers, cheese, jellies, notepaper, snack foods, bath oil, and so one have been included. My grandmothers look forward to these packages every year.

Susan Colwell resides in Windsor, New York.

CHRISTMAS CARD TREE

One year we had just moved in and were unable to unpack our Christmas tree decorations. As Christmas cards arrived at our home, we would punch a hole in the corner of each one, slip a ribbon through the hole, and tie the card to the Christmas tree. You could still read the cards and the tree looked so pretty!

Nancy Price resides in Brooksville, Florida.

MAYFLOWER BASKETS

Let the children decorate a basket. Fill the basket with goodies that an elderly friend could use:

- Canned Food
- Fruit
- Nuts
- Stationery
- Stamps
- Assorted cards (birthday, get well)

TRADITIONS TO MAKE

Take the basket to an elderly friend or neighbor. Put the basket on the doorknob or by the door. Ring the door bell and hide!*

CREATE YOUR OWN NATIVITY SCENE

Each Christmas we pull out a very special nativity scene. It would win no art contest. The little play dough figures look the worse for wear. One angel had a broken wing and her halo is lost. The camel only has three toothpick legs. The wise men have long ago lost their gifts. But it still gets center stage at our house. Why? Because it is one of our most special holiday memories and traditions.

It all started one holiday season years ago when the three boys were bored and hyper. We were temporarily living in the U.S., and our Christmas decorations, including our nativity scene, were packed away at our home in Austria. With more time than money or talent, we decided to create our own nativity scene.

Using the Creative Clay recipe that follows, we molded our little people. They somewhat resembled little Fisher Price people, just a little more (or perhaps a lot more) rustic! We let them dry and then painted each with tempera paints. The following Saturday we took a walk through the woods and picked up anything of interest, such as moss, roots, acorns, sticks, stones, and pine cones. We brought our "treasures" home, and on a piece of plywood, we constructed our very own nativity scene. The manger was crafted from a root covered with moss. Pine cones served as trees. The final touch was adding our little nativity people

Used by permission of Thomas Nelson, Inc., Publishers.

and animals that we had made from the play dough. When we returned to our home in Austria, we took our little people along. Each year we took a family walk in the woods picking up goodies, and later at home we reconstructed our manger scene. How special it has been each Christmas to bring out our little homemade nativity people —broken wings, broken legs, and all. They bring back great memories of Christmases past.

So when boredom threatens to strike at your home, pull out the play dough recipe. Make your own nativity people, take your own walk in the woods, assemble your own simple nativity scene, and add to your family's special Christmas memories.

Creative Clay

1 cup cornstarch	2 cups baking soda
1 1/4 cups cold water	(1-pound package)

Stir the cornstarch and baking soda together. Mix in cold water and stir over medium heat until the mixture has the consistency of mashed potatoes. Turn onto a plate and cover with a damp cloth until cool enough to handle. Then knead. Use immediately or store in an airtight container.*

Dave and Claudia Arp

THE TWELVE DAYS OF CHRISTMAS

Do you want to send a very unique and unusual Christmas present to a family you love? Let us tell you about a memory-building gift we received from our dear friends,

---

Used by permission of Thomas Nelson, Inc., Publishers.

the Peddicords. They sent us "The Twelve Days of Christmas." As we opened the Christmas box, the first thing we saw was a book of Christmas carols with this note:

> *Sing the song on Page 26 before opening this present or sharing it with others. Sit together and have time without other distractions too, if possible. We're thinking of you this Christmas!*
> *Love, Clark and Ann*

You guessed it! The song was "The Twelve Days of Christmas," and in the box were twelve gifts to be opened. Each was numbered so we knew how to proceed, and each represented one of the twelve days of Christmas. Why not have some fun this year and send "The Twelve Days of Christmas" to a family you know. Use your imagination. Here are some suggestions to get you started.

- •Day 1: a partridge in a pear tree—This could be "home-made art" drawn by one of the children.
- •Day 2: two turtle doves—Our friends sent a small framed picture of two birds that is still on our memento shelf.
- •Day 3: three French hens—Make three chicken Christmas tree ornaments out of felt.
- •Day 4: four calling birds—Draw a picture of four birds all talking on the telephone.
- •Day 5: five golden rings—Make five gold napkin rings out of felt. Simply cut in strips (2 inches by 6 inches) and sew the short ends together.
- •Day 6: six geese a-laying—What about six chocolate eggs?

We've gotten you started. On the last six, you're on your own.

- Day 7:   seven swans a-swimming
- Day 8:   eight maids a-milking
- Day 9:   nine ladies dancing
- Day 10: ten lords a-leaping
- Day 11: eleven pipers piping
- Day 12: twelve drummers drumming

Wrap the gifts individually, label them, and send this unique gift on its way. Be sure to include a copy of the song, "The Twelve Days of Christmas," and a note suggesting that they set aside at least thirty minutes to an hour to open and enjoy your gift. Then sit back and wait for their happy response!*

Dave and Claudia Arp are the founders of Marriage Alive International, a worldwide ministry. Currently they write a column for Christian Parenting Today *magazine and host a two-minute radio program,* "The Family Workshop."

AN EASY ADVENT CALENDAR

My two-year-old daughter and I made our own Advent calendar last year and it didn't cost us anything. Take a large piece of cardboard and paint a large evergreen tree, almost to the edges of cardboard. Punch two holes in the top of the cardboard with a paper punch and tie a red ribbon through holes to hang it on the wall. We then sorted through old Christmas cards and cut out small pictures.

Used by permission of Thomas Nelson, Inc., Publishers.

Christmas dolls, candles, snowflakes, sleighs, bells, angels, stars, candy canes, and so on are some examples. Put these in an envelope. Each day, starting on 1 December, Rachel and I would get out the envelope and spread out several cut-out pictures. Rachel would pick out one and we would then glue it on the tree wherever she wanted. She loved doing the Advent calendar and always reminded me before breakfast each day.

Mary Jane Allio resides in Tionesta, Pennsylvania.

THE TOUCH-IT TREE

The year our first child was two years old, I let her help me decorate the family Christmas tree. When we finished, I had a small two-foot artificial tree I had purchased with nonbreakable decorations, most of them homemade. She and I put "her" tree up and then I explained that she could not touch the big tree because it was just to look at, but she could touch her tree and do what she wanted with it.

That evening her daddy came home and she grabbed his hand to take him in to view the trees. Pointing to the family tree, she said, "Don't touch it, Daddy." Then she pointed to her tree and said, "That's the Touch-It Tree."

From that holiday on, until our family had grown and moved away to college, we had a Touch-It Tree. The decorations changed as our children grew older but it was always their tree to put up and do with as they wished. As little children they often dragged it around the house, putting it up and taking it down many times during December, but they never touched the big tree and never broke an ornament on the big tree. When they were old enough they made their own ornaments, and one year all of the ornaments were edible. This is a tradition that will be carried on in their families when they have children because it was so special for them.

Judy Lovitt resides in Ogden, Utah.

GRANDMA'S ORNAMENTS

Christmas celebrations always bring to mind a rush of memories. Each memory is as individual as the year it was created, and all are cherished reminders of days gone by.

Some years ago my mother struck upon an idea for making each year a special celebration for her grandchildren. She purchases for each one a personalized, dated tree ornament. Sometimes the ornaments represent the child's interest or hobby and sometimes they are all alike, representing something special to the giver.

The children always look forward to "Grandma's ornaments" and it's every bit as much fun for my mother.

When it comes time to decorate the Christmas tree, we make a special event of it with eggnog and goodies. We pull out dusty boxes of Christmas decorations and as we sort through the ornaments the memories come to life. "I remember when. . ." is probably the most often-heard phrase of the day.

While we join together to celebrate the birth of our Lord, we celebrate not only the family He's blessed us with but the memories of our lives together. I believe it's the love we have through Him for one another, as well as the good and bad times we've shared, that makes us a family.

When our children grow up and leave home, I want them to take not only "Grandma's ornaments," but eighteen or more years of memories of celebrating a family Christmas.

Tracie J. Peterson is a regular columnist for a Christian newspaper as well as a writer of inspirational romances (Heartsong Presents, Bethany House Publishers). She resides in Topeka, Kansas.

AN ORNAMENTAL CENTERPIECE

Make a pretty decoration by filling a clear glass bowl with glass Christmas ornaments and a string of either colored or clear tiny lights. Add a few sprigs of green on top to complete a delightful decoration for a cupboard or centerpiece (use battery operated lights).

Here's a variation of that idea. Before the Christmas dinner have a glass ornament on each plate with an empty glass bowl in the center of the table. Each person around the table then tells one thing that he or she is thankful for and places the ornament in the bowl.

Kathy Offord resides in Barron, Wisconsin.

CHRISTMAS DINNER GIFTS

Small packages are placed on the plates at the beginning of our Christmas dinner. These gifts are chosen wit the intention of bringing our minds back to Christ after a busy season of excitement, shopping, and gift giving.

Among our favorite gifts have been small heart paper clips that told of Jesus' love, name-bearing bookmarks with Scriptures for each person, and polished rocks in small Christmas stockings. Along with the rock each person got a Scripture telling how Christ is our Rock. After reading the Scriptures aloud each person was encouraged to keep his rock in a pocket or coin purse as a reminder that we can rely on the Lord.

Sylvia Stone resides in Medical Lake, Washington.

THE FAMILY TREE

When my children finished high school and college, I cross-stitched graduation caps with names, dates, and schools and made ornaments for the tree. I also made ornaments from pictures of the children in Santa's lap and of grandparents who are no longer with us a good memory of Christmases past. Now my grandson will learn of his family tree from our Christmas tree.

Mildred S. Barton resides in Anderson, South Carolina.

"PROMISE" STOCKING STUFFERS

When times were tough and money was scarce, we began a tradition that each family member still looks forward to every Christmas.

For each family member with a stocking hanging at the fireplace, prepare one personal promise. A simple pledge to perform some duty can be scratched on a 3 x 5 card and inserted by the promisor, who signs his or her name at the bottom. Promises can be used like certificates, redeemable during the new year, by simply pulling out the "coupon" and collecting on the promise.

Promises may be for attitude changes, chores, special occasions, just use your imagination! Some samples of promises might include the following:

- One foot rub
- I'll do your kitchen duty
- One movie night, popcorn and all
- I will clean up my room, no arguments
- I promise to be more thankful
- Date night: You choose the spot
- I'll wash the dog (or the car, and so on)
- I'll make lunches in the morning
- I give you the day off: no housework,
    no homework—relaxation of your choice
- Read a book with you (for a little one)
- One free manicure

These very personal gift certificates are a special way of saying you care. (The trick is to keep them where you can find them again!) It's always a special moment when, in emptying the stockings, we all share our promises, and revel in the thought we can redeem the coupon in a desperate time of need!

SURPRISE CALENDAR

A special gift Grandma or Grandpa would cherish from their grandchildren, or grandparents can prepare for parents of small children. The calendar picture for each month is personalized for the recipient!

During the year plan to get together with family members and ask each one to draw a picture that represents a calendar month. They may be scribbled in crayon, smeared in watercolor, scratched in pencil, or more professionally rendered by an older family member. Just be sure all twelve pictures are on the same size paper (8 1/2 x 11 inches or larger) and each one represents a particular month. A special family occasion could even be pictured: a wedding anniversary, birthday, graduation, and so on. Here are some other suggestions:

January:	Snowpeople, winter clothes
February:	Presidents' birthdays, valentines
March:	Wind, spring flowers breaking through
April:	Easter events, lilies, church
May:	Maypole, Memorial Day, Mother's Day
June:	Father's Day, graduation
July:	American flags, summer fun
August:	Hot summer days, out-of-school activities
September:	Back to school, Labor Day
October:	Fall leaves, colors
November:	Thanksgiving turkey, Indians, pilgrims
December:	Christmas memories and fun

After October the new year's calendars are available. Purchase any one in which your pictures will fit (if the picture space is larger, just paste up on construction paper background). Glue your personalized pictures over the printed ones and wrap up for a special Christmas gift. The children who helped create the calendar will be excited because most likely they've long forgotten the picture they drew. What a splendid way to remind a special someone they are loved, every month of the year!

Lee Ezell is a well-known author and speaker on women's issues. Among her books are The Cinderella Syndrome, *(Bantom Books, Inc.) and* The Missing Piece, *(Servant).*

RECYCLED CARDS

As our Christmas cards arrive, my little girl opens them and then we read and tape them on the door. After New Year's Day I go through and cut them on the folded edge. The sides with the picture I save. Some are appropriate to use to write on the back and send in an envelope as thank yous for Christmas gifts. Others are usable as Christmas postcards for next year or for various craft projects. Finally, some I send to St. Jude's Ranch for Children where the fronts of cards are recycled (100 St. Jude's Street, Boulder City, NV 89005).

Mary Jane Allio resides in Tionesta, Pennsylvania.

ADVENT PRAYER CHAIN

Here's an idea for a Sunday school class, large extended family, or neighborhood. Make an Advent prayer chain for each household, writing prayer concerns on colored strips of construction paper. Class members or family or friends write the same concern on twenty-eight (or fewer) pieces of paper so that each night prayers are being raised for specific concerns. Join the chains together and rejoice in being faithful in prayer for someone you care about.

Andy Caughey resides in Harrington Park, New Jersey.

THE JESUS TREE

On the first day of December we put up a "Jesus Tree." The tree is made of green felt and is placed on the refrigerator with magnets. Each night our two sons tape ornaments also made of felt on the tree. They choose one type of ornament to place on the tree and continue each night until all ornaments are on the tree. We have made about twenty of each ornament and each type has its own significance. The ornaments include the following:

Mangers:	to show how Jesus was born
Crosses:	to show how Jesus died
Blood Drops:	to show He shed His blood for us
Candlesticks:	to signify Jesus is the Light of the World
Stars:	He is the bright and morning star (also the star led the wise men)
Bibles:	God's Holy Word and Jesus is the Word
Lambs:	Jesus is the Lamb of God
Bread:	Jesus is the Bread of Life

Because the tree is quite visible and different, visitors to our home ask about it. We explain the ornaments, enabling us to witness to our friends. The Jesus Tree is our way of keeping Christ in Christmas.

The Mike Hill Family resides in Ripley, Mississippi.

GIFTS FROM JESUS

Although we put our tree up the first part of December, we stack all presents by the piano. Under the tree we place all the presents that Jesus gives to us.

We take wooden blocks of assorted sizes (scraps from 2 x 4, 2 x 6, 2 x 12 lumber) and cover them with white butcher paper (wrap like presents). Each day we take one and write on the outside something that Jesus gives us (forgiveness, inner peace, strength, and so on). We rotate days so a different family member gets to name a present at least once a week.

When Christmas arrives we have a thank-you prayer, thanking the Lord for all the presents He has given us. Our tree is overflowing with presents and our hearts are overflowing with thankfulness.

A THANK-YOU BOX

This is a special heartfelt present for you to give to Jesus. Take and cover a shoebox with wrapping paper. Cover the lid separately so you can open it without unwrapping.

On a piece of paper write a thank-you note to Jesus for something specific He has done for you. Fill the box with thank-you notes and read them occasionally during the season when things get hectic. Keep it handy all year long and fill it with thank yous. By next Christmas you'll need a bigger box!

Diane Armstrong resides in Sedro-Woolley, Washington.

WHAT'S A SWEETSWAP?

For several years we have had a Christmas "Sweetswap" at our church where six to eight couples exchange Christmas ornaments and cookies. The twist to it is that each *wife* hand-made the ornaments and each *husband* makes the cookies from scratch, each *with absolutely no help from the other!* If there are eight couples involved, each wife is responsible for providing seven handmade ornaments and each husband is to provide seven dozen homemade cookies.

We meet in a home after Sunday evening service about two weeks prior to Christmas. Each couple brings a covered dish to share along with their exchange items. After snacking and socializing, the ornaments and dozens of cookies are exchanged, usually in little decorative sacks or plates with the ornaments attached. The husband shares any bits of wisdom or humor he encountered as he made his cookies, and those listening offer their comments concerning the appearance of his delicacies.

Everyone looks forward to this very fun evening. There is a lot of "ribbing" and good clean Christian fun shared during the evening.

As a plus, we now ask that each couple bring an extra dozen cookies and an ornament and we invite the minister and his wife to come and enjoy the fun. Their ticket in, rather than come empty-handed, is to bring a covered dish to share.

Marilyn Pfeifer resides in Washington C. H., Ohio.

LUMINARIAS

These French paper lanterns, called *lampions*, can be made by youngsters to make your entry say "welcome." Make your own luminaria bags from sturdy glossy paper or from simple brown paper lunch bags. In either case, fold and make cut-outs in the bag to let light show through. You may glue colored tissue paper inside to diffuse the light and give a stained-glass effect, or you can leave the bag as it is. For each bag you'll need a glass jar. Put some sand in the bottom of the jar and a votive candle on top of the sand. Luminarias should last for many holiday nights.*

*From 101 Ideas for the Best-Ever Christmas. *Copyright 1992 by Caryl Waller Krueger. Excerpted by permission of the publisher, Abingdon Press.*

CHRISTMAS LONG AGO

Grandparents can make very special cards for their grandchildren by sharing what Christmas was like in their youth. Type or write these memories and then glue them onto colored paper folders. Make a different one for each child in the family.*

MEMORY CANDLES

Almost forty years ago when we were living in the Belgian Congo (now Zaire) the idea came to me to save memories by melting the remnants of birthday and Christmas candles and making one candle to represent the whole year. That first candle wasn't very large. A small fruit juice can was more than adequate to hold the melted wax from three sets of birthday candles, my husband's, our daughter's, and mine, and the few stubs of red and green Christmas candles that we didn't save for the next year. When it was unmolded it stood about three inches high.

As years passed we added three more birthdays and each one yielded more candles. When we returned to the United States to live, I was quicker to discard used candles. There were other festive occasions, like wedding anniversaries, graduations, and prom parties, which provided candles, so my memory candles grew bigger.

Each year thereafter we brought out our memory candles early in December and arranged them on the piano.

*From 101 Ideas for the Best-Ever Christmas. Copyright 1992 by Caryl Waller Krueger. Excerpted by permission of the publisher, Abingdon Press.

Christmas Eve we lighted them and enjoyed their glow while we sang carols and read the Christmas story.

When it was time to leave our home and move into a retirement complex, I stopped making candles. I considered remelting all the candles and making just one big one but my daughters didn't like that idea.

They picked out the ones with special memories for them—wedding year, graduation, first baby's birthday—and then they divided the others. Today the candles are set out in their homes, and one daughter has continued the tradition of making her own candle each year.

When I picture all those candles lighted and the family sitting around them singing "Joy to the World," the memories return, just as precious as when I first melted a few wax remnants and poured them into a glass.

Margaret S. Jump resides in Lewisburg, Pennsylvania.

COOKIE CUTTER FRAMES

Preserve Christmas memories and build an ornament collection at the same time! Select your favorite cutter shape as well as a cherished photo of your child from that year. Simply trim the photo to size and glue the edges to the cookie cutter. Decorate with ribbon, paint, and glitter as desired. Remember to date the back of the photo for an accurate recording of your child's growing-up years.

MORE STOCKINGS

One of my favorite funny but practical gifts to give is a fluffy red Christmas stocking stuffed with. . .what else?

Stockings!
>   *Janet LaSpina resides in Dunmore, Pennsylvania.*

A GALLERY OF GREETINGS

Each year we select the greeting card we like best from those received and frame it. We date the framed card and include the address and name of the sender in order to identify later on. Through the years we have accumulated quite a gallery of Christmas scenes. These framed cards are displayed along with our other holiday decorations each year.

>   *Valeria Richard resides in Escatawpa, Mississippi.*

PEACH TEA MIX IN A BAG

1 cup instant tea mix   1 box peach gelatin
2 cups granulated sugar

Combine all ingredients in a large bowl; mix well. Store in an airtight container. To serve, stir about 2 teaspoons tea mix into 8 ounces hot water.

If given as a gift, put the mixture into an airtight plastic bag and make a fabric bag as a covering.

To make a fabric bag, cut a 7x23-inch piece of fabric. With right sides together, sew sides of bag together. Turn bag right side out, turn top edge of bag under 1/4-inch and topstitch. Tie two 18-inch pieces of ribbon in a bow around the bag. For a more festive touch, tuck a sprig of holly under the bow. Include inside a card with serving instructions.

>   *Sharyn Bischof resides in Bridgeview, Illinois.*

POTPOURRI BAG TREE ORNAMENTS

1 small rubber band   4 x 6 inches fancy lace
10 inches of 1/4-inch ribbon,   1/2 cup potpourri
  (color coordinated with lace)

Take a 4x6-inch piece of fancy lace for each bag. With right sides together, sew sides of bag, leaving top and bottom sides open. Turn right side out and stitch across bottom above fancy border so it is free flowing. Fill with potpourri of your choice. Take the ribbon and weave it in and out around the top. Take the small rubber band and wrap it around the top to keep potpourri in the bag. Pull ribbon tight so it looks like a small handbag. Hang it on your tree! (When you take down your tree, store potpourri in an airtight plastic bag. Potpourri bags can be refreshed yearly as needed.)

Rhonda Gwara resides in Rome, New York.

WISHBONE ORNAMENTS

My mother seemed to always find ways to add to our family fun. At Thanksgiving she would set aside the turkey's wishbone, wash it, and let it dry. Then she would show us children how to wrap it with aluminum foil. When it was time to trim our Christmas tree, we looped thread or a thin ribbon to the top of the wishbone, and hung it on our tree. As the years went by, we added more and more glistening wishbones to our lucky-looking Christmas tree.

Charlotte Adelsperger resides in Overland Park, Kansas.

TRADITIONS TO SHARE

HOW TO KEEP HOLIDAYS STRESSLESS

1. Ask your family members to share their favorite holiday memory. You may be surprised how few meals and toys they mention. We did this at our church Christmas party one year and, to my surprise, very few of the recall special holiday memories. If this be the case, create some memories. Make your time count—a memory lasts forever, but toys get broken.

2. Try not to do everything yourself. Small children can help, just lower your perfection a little and allow those small hands to bake and decorate. These experiences may stay in their memories long after the holidays are over. Even if your husband is unable to help you the rest of the year, the Christmas spirit will inspire him. Ask him to help you or ask if he could run some errands near where he works.

3. Settle family matters ahead of the holiday time. Families are often separated by divorce or geographic distance and disputes can arise. Try to make all the arrangements well ahead of time. If you have out of town guests, decide where they will stay and let them know before they arrive if they really need to be at a motel. Share your time equally and fairly with each set of grandparents or take turns from year to year. Avoid overcommitment—it can make for situations where people are overtired and overreact.

4. Don't gain weight. Feeling fat in party clothes can really add to your stress and tension. Overeating can make you feel absolutely awful. Try to schedule the same exercise you normally do. If you are not exercising now make

it a goal for the new year.

There will be a great deal of extra goodies around, but be selective about what you eat. Stick to the things that are worth it, like your favorites that you see only at holiday time.

Place yourself next to the food table where the fruit or veggie platter is. If you decide now not to overdo it, you won't have to make that New Year's resolution to lose weight later.

5. Remember what really matters. As Christians, Christmas is the time for celebrating the birth of Christ and everything else comes after that special celebration. The hassles will take care of themselves.

6. Watch your finances carefully. Talk about tension and depression! Overspending will do it especially if you've overcharged and have those bills to look forward to later. Ask the Lord to help you in this area so you won't get caught up in the spirit of things and buy much more than you budgeted for.

Remember that a handmade gift or baked item can be more valuable than an expensive one. Special phone calls or a coupon for an "after Christmas lunch treat" can mean as much to a friend as an expensive gift they may not use or like. Set your budget and stick to it. Many people have a special Christmas fund set aside. That makes it easy and when that's gone, it's gone. Otherwise, spread your purchases over a period of time and charge only the amount you intend to spend. That's why we suggest you begin your gift shopping early in November so it doesn't all come at once.

7. It's okay to say no. You'd like to do it all, be everywhere, and see everything. But for today's busy woman, it just can't be. Don't be afraid to say, "No, we need this time

together as a family" or "No, I can't bake the extra cookies but I'd be happy to buy some." Don't feel guilty about those things you simply can't do.

8. Plan some time for yourself. You can read a book, listen to a tape or music, take a bubble bath with a candle lit, get a good haircut, have your nails polished, or maybe even buy yourself a new nightgown, blouse, or holiday sweater. By taking care of yourself, that last-minute hassle about your appearance won't happen.

9. Christmas will come regardless if you've done everything on your lists or not. Do those things which really matter and let the others fall where they may.

Family, friends, and above all the true meaning of Christmas is what counts. Remember 60 percent of our stress is caused by disorganization.*

Emilie Barnes is a noted speaker, seminar leader, and author. More Hours in My Day and The Spirit of Loveliness (Harvest House Publishers) are among her best-known books.

A THANKSGIVING PRAYER

We have been painfully aware in recent years that two special people are now absent from the family circle, Jim's father and my uncle. . . . I am reminded at this moment of a prayer expressed by Jim's father during the final year of his life. . . .

Excerpt from: The Complete Holiday Organizer by Emilie Barnes. Copyright 1987 by Harvest House Publishers, Eugene, Oregon 97402. Used by permission.

He said, "Lord, we have enjoyed being together so much this past week, and you have been good to make this time possible. But Lord, we are realistic enough to know that life moves on, and that circumstances will not always be as we enjoy them today. We understand that a day is coming when the fellowship we now share will be but a memory to those who remain. That's why I want to thank you for bringing love into our lives for this season, and for the happiness we have experienced with one another."

. . .Circumstances will inevitably change; nothing in this life is eternal or permanent. But while God grants us breath, we will enjoy one another to the fullest and spread our love as far and wide as possible.

Thanksgiving at the Dobson home is an occasion for the celebration of that philosophy.*

Shirley Dobson is the chairman of the National Day of Prayer and serves on the Board of Directors of the Focus on the Family Ministry. She is married to psychologist and best-selling author Dr. James C. Dobson.

THE TWELVE SURPRISES OF CHRISTMAS

As a take-off of this theme, my young son chooses twelve people whom he feels should receive special gifts during the twelve days leading up to Christmas. These gifts are often handmade and are not given in the spirit that something will be received in return. Sometimes we choose a person we don't know, maybe living in a nursing home,

---

Let's Make a Memory, Gloria Gaither and Shirley Dobson, Copyright 1983, Word, Inc., Dallas, Texas. Used by permission.

to be the recipient of such a gift. The real joy in this is the lesson of sharing that it teaches all of us.

Nancy Price resides in Brooksville, Florida.

A LIGHT IN THE DARKNESS

Christians know Advent, a word which means "coming," as a time of preparation and reflection. For the course of four Sundays preceding Christmas Eve, a period of twenty-two to twenty-eight days, we anticipate celebrating the birth of Christ.

Scripture readings for Advent center around the prophecy of a Messiah and His birth in Bethlehem. They tell, too, of our life together in His name, and of His promise to return as reigning King and judge of the world.

Advent is like a light in the darkness. For us it will always be a time of great hope. A King called Immanuel has come into our midst, and "He will save His people from their sins."

The Advent wreath represents God's never-ending love and eternity, and the surrounding evergreens, the four Sundays. Set among the evergreens are the four candles of Advent: the first, the Candle of Light; the second, the Candle of Hope; the third, the Candle of Joy; and on the fourth Sunday the Candle of Love is lit. A fifth candle in the center of the wreath, called the Christ Candle, is lit on Christmas Eve or Christmas Day to represent the bright light of the Messiah, Jesus, who declared, "I am the Light of the world."

Fred A. Hartley serves as pastor at the Lilburn Alliance Church, Lilburn, Georgia. He is also a popular author, as demonstrated by The Teenage Book of Manners. . .PLEASE! *(Barbour Publishing, Inc.).*

THE SPIRIT OF GIVING

A few years ago while planning a Christmas party with my junior high girls' Sunday school class, the students asked if they could exchange gifts, something I'd discouraged in past years. Some of my students lived in the inner city and came on the church buses; I knew that any extra expense around Christmas would be a burden to their families.

However, I didn't want to squelch the spirit of giving, and I remembered what great fun it was to exchange gifts at school or Sunday school as a child. "All right," I finally said. "But here are the rules. You may not spend more than one dollar on the gift that you bring."

"A dollar!" cried several girls in unison, as if they'd practiced it. "What can you buy for that?" wailed another. I wondered, then, if perhaps my idea hadn't been so good, but I wasn't about to back down. After all, it's the thought that should be important when giving or getting a gift, not how much was spent—and setting such a strict limit would insure that the girls gave some thought to their gifts.

"It can be something you buy, or make," I told them, hoping that my show of enthusiasm would be contagious. "And at the party, we'll display the gifts you brought after they're opened. Just don't cheat—keep the price under a dollar."

There were no more protests, and I knew I had them when a girl raised her hand and asked, "Does that include tax?"

"You may go over a dollar to pay sales tax. Any questions?" There were no questions, so in my best imitation of a football coach I said, "I want to see some creativity, whether you buy or make the gift. Class dismissed."

Three weeks later our party was held in the fellowship hall of the church. I was anxious to see how the girls had done with their assignment. After we drew names and swapped gifts, each student, one at a time, stood and displayed what she'd been given. And how clever the girls had been! One of the gifts was a simple cardboard earring box, covered with velvet, lace, and fake pearls. A couple of girls had made fancy hair ribbons. Store-bought gifts included a diary, lip gloss, and fun things like bubble bath.

Best of all was how much the class enjoyed it. "Can we do it again next year?" several girls asked me. "You bet!" was my reply.

Kate Blackwell is a popular writer of inspirational romance who resides in Baton Rouge, Louisiana. Among her recent books is Shores of Deliverance (*Heartsong Presents*).

PROJECT ANGEL TREE®

My family decided to broaden our gift giving by sharing with those with greater physical needs. We set aside a designated amount of money and purchased gifts for the families of prisoners through Project Angel Tree®. Our daughter helped pick out toys, clothes, books, candy, and more. We all wrapped the gifts and included in each a tract and a telephone number if there are questions. The gifts are then delivered to families by Project Angel Tree® workers.*

Jan DePasqualin resides in Allen Park, Michigan.

---

* For further information on Project Angel Tree®, a Ministry of Prison Fellowship, telephone toll-free (800) 398-HOPE or (703) 478-0100, extension 634.

GIVING FOR FUN

Throughout the year our two children, ages five and seven, receive $1.50 allowance each week. Fifty cents of their allowance is theirs to keep and spend, fifty cents is their church contribution, and fifty cents goes into their "savings" banks. At Christmastime, they take their year's savings and purchase gifts.

Last year, after everything was said and done, our daughter gave me a big hug and said, "You know, Mommy, it sure is fun giving presents to people!" My prayer is that in this age of self-gratification my children will learn that it is truly more blessed to give than to receive.

Tina Briley resides in Corpus Christi, Texas.

SEASONAL SEESAW

I love the holidays! I hate the holidays! I am a Christmas contradiction. I'm up with excitement and then down with disappointment. I'm up with anticipation and then down with depression. I'm up with . . .well, you get the idea. I'm on my seasonal seesaw. My teeter-totter partner is my own Currier-and-Ives expectations.

Ever notice in those Currier and Ives pictures how even in frigid weather the cows are contented? They willingly pose next to the wood for the fireplace, which is neatly stacked next to the house. While Bossy grins, Junior is shown joyfully skipping out to bring Mother dear kindling for the stove.

I don't have a cow, but I do have a dog. Pumpkin refuses to go outside if it's damp. She has an aversion to moist feet. She will sit for days with her paws crossed, waiting for the sun or wind to dry up the ground. No way is she going to pose willingly by a wet wood pile.

Of course, that would be difficult anyway since we don't have any wood—that is, unless I hike five miles to the woods and gnaw off a few branches. Oh, well, our fireplace stays cleaner that way.

I tried to imagine our Junior skipping joyfully toward a task outside in inclement weather. Ha! I think Junior caught Pumpkins's malady.

No matter how I try, I can't seem to cram my family onto the front of one of those cards.

I don't know why I can't remember, from one Christmas season to the next, that Currier and Ives is an unattainable height. Every Christmas, I want my house to be picture perfect. Ha! I can't achieve that in a nonholiday time, much less in a season with so many added demands.

I imagine white birch logs (cut by me in our back 40— feet, that is) snuggled in a handwoven basket (I designed) placed next to the hearth. The blazing fire invites guest to warm in our candle-lit (all hand-dipped by me) dining room. I would serve a gourmet dinner for thirty, followed by strolling musicians playing Handel's "Messiah." All this would take place in my 10-by-12 dining area.

When I have such unreasonable goals, I end up with a high frustration level and a frazzled nervous system. Then I find myself in last-minute panic spurts, trying to excuse, hide, and disguise all my unfinished projects.

One year we decided to write "Noel" in lights on our house. We started late and finished only half the project because of bad weather. That left a multi-colored NO flashing on our rooftop. We had fewer guests that year.

Usually, I wait too long to complete my shopping, leaving me victim to jangled nerves from holiday traffic, crowds, and check-out lines. People's personalities are seldom enhanced under pressure. Also, I tend to be more impulsive in my buying when I'm running late. I suffer from bargain whiplash trying to take advantage of all the Christmas markdowns. Too many last-minute purchases leave me holding the bag. . .and it's full of bills. The bills then pile up in my emotions, leaving me feeling spent.

Also, during the holiday hoopla I seem to get bit by the bug. No, not the flu bug; the love bug. I fall into the trap of thinking everyone is going to get along. Give me a break! How unrealistic to believe relatives and friends, some of whom have never hit if off, would suddenly become seasonal sidekicks! I'm learning there are those who believe "Ho, Ho, Ho" is something you do strictly in your garden and has nothing to do with exhibiting a merry heart.

Another habit I have is wanting everyone to love the gifts I give them as much as I did when I selected them. I'm into applause and appreciation. Here's the problems: I live with three guys (one husband and two sons), and they only applaud silly things like grand slam home runs in the World Series, touchdowns in the final seconds of the Super Bowl, or when I fix dinner and they can tell what it is.

They don't show the same enthusiasm for my gifts— like the nifty button extenders, the monogrammed electric socks, or the fuschsia-colored long johns I wrapped for them. I realize my gifts are. . .uh. . .distinctive, but I want them to be memorable. My guys agree they have been.

Well, there it is, my Christmas confession. Maybe some of you can identify with part, if not all, of my seasonal seesaw. Come join me in entering into the holidays without the teeter and totter in our emotions. Here's how:

1. Set more-sane house goals. Better to plan less and accomplish more than to fall short of your ideal and start your holidays feeling disappointed.

2. Shop early, and buy a couple of generic emergency gifts. (Unlike fuchsia underwear, a box of fine chocolates holds general appeal.)

3. Settle on a reasonable budget before going into the stores to prevent falling victim to strong sales tactics (which include Christmas mood music that plays on our nostalgia, sale-sign seduction, and plastic explosives in the form of credit cards).

4. Sow the seeds of goodwill, but don't expect every "Scrooge" in your Christmas circle to embrace your efforts . . .or you, for that matter. Don't snowball your own emotions by expecting love from people who can't give it. (History in a relationship is usually a good benchmark of his or her ability.)

5. Seek some silence. Balance your busyness with moments of meditation. Don't allow all the flashing lights on the outside to distract you from the inner light of His presence. Even a short silence each day will give a greater semblance of order to your emotions and schedule.

Set goals, shop early, settle budget, sow goodwill,
seek silence,
and don't forget to SIMPLY CELEBRATE!

Ways to celebrate simply

Make a snow angel, drink eggnog, write a forgotten friend, decorate a snowman, go caroling in your neighborhood, feed the birds, bake apples, watch the movies *Heidi* and *Little Women*, write a poem, cut out cookies, share tea with a friend, frame an old snapshot, hug a child, hug an oldster, read the Christmas story out loud, and sing *Happy Birthday* to Jesus.*

Patsy Clairmont is a popular speaker and best-selling author of God Uses Cracked Pots *(Focus on the Family Publishing). She resides in Brighton, Michigan.*

REMEMBER YOUR MISSIONARIES

Instead of using postage to send cards to church members, our church sets up boxes in the foyer divided into sections for each letter of the alphabet. Members hand out cards there, and check for cards for themselves as well. Everyone is encouraged to use the postage money they would have spent for the missionary offering.

Adopt two or three (or more!) missionary families from your church and write them during this season. They often feel the most lonely for their families and their country when they are gone over the holidays. Choose families that have children about your own children's ages and have your children include notes or pictures.

Michelle C. Hooks resides in Apopka, Florida.

WHO WILL MAKE THE LIGHTS SPARKLE?

When I was a child, I thought Christmas never came soon enough. I anxiously awaited the first set of lights to appear or for the smell of pine as my grandfather carried in

---

*Reprinted with permission from Normal Is Just a Setting On Your Dryer, *by Focus on the Family Publishing. Copyright 1993, Patsy Clairmont.*

the still-growing evergreen tree for us to decorate. Every moment was magic and it made the lights sparkle.

I never dreamed that Christmas could become a chore, a drudgery, and a burden, but that is exactly what happened when I became a parent and—not by choice—the family's "Christmas magician."

Suddenly it was up to me to decorate our home, bake cookies, buy and wrap the perfect gift for everyone, address and write witty Christmas cards, and then wait breathlessly for the season to arrive. And trust me—I was out of breath, and out of joy and excitement, for the holiday I had always loved best.

Christmas had become a major production that began six months ahead of time. Christmas decorations were on sale along with the back-to-school supplies. We hurried through Halloween and almost ignored Thanksgiving. The Christmas rush started earlier and earlier each year.

I watched the crowds as they circled the malls draped in silver and tinsel, with Elvis Christmas carols booming, and I never saw a smiling face. I know the shepherds came with haste but I don't believe they meant to create the Christmas rush.

I'd buy every holiday publication offered at the newsstands. Yes, I did want to make those lace angels and red velvet bows to redo the three this year. Yes, I could frost our gingerbread house to look like Disney World. Why I bet I could even needlepoint all eight reindeer on coasters in time. And I'd order Christmas tree toilet paper. That was just the right touch.

Touched is right—I was losing my mind. I'd work all hours of the night so that everything would be perfect. After all, I could sleep in January. I could never understand why my husband didn't get more (or even somewhat) enthusiastic about the holidays. Okay, so I was exhausted and grumpy, the kids were on a sugar high, and we were broke. Did that give him any right to be downright negative?

When I read about a workshop called "How to Deal with Christmas Stress" I said, "Enough is enough!" Christmas stress should be a contradiction in terms. I evaluated how we were observing the birth of a child born in a very humble stable. We had lost sight of what was meaningful and important. I wanted to see Christmas through the eyes of a child again. I wanted the lights to sparkle.

Then I found a book, *Unplug the Christmas Machine*, that has since changed the way my family approaches and celebrates Christmas. It is full of ideas about how to return to a simpler, more joy-filled holiday.

Ninety percent of what we do at Christmas is for children. But, contrary to popular belief, kids do not want a perfect Victorian tree, a formal dinner party, or exhausted, frantic parents.

According to *Unplug the Christmas Machine*, they want:

1. Relaxed and loving time with the family.
2. Realistic expectations about gifts.
3. An evenly paced holiday season.
4. Strong family traditions.

So now our family is striving to make some gradual changes and restructure our Christmas. We love our families dearly but we were going to four different celebrations on Christmas Eve and Christmas Day. Inevitably, the first snow or ice storm hit right about then so we'd often be taking our lives in our hands.

Now we've asked one side of the family to celebrate a day or two after Christmas, and we visit with just one family on Christmas Day. That leaves Christmas Eve for our children's Christmas program and a candlelight buffet at home with just our own family. It's a new tradition that we treasure.

Another aspect of Christmas has often disturbed me. What do we give our children for Christmas gifts? The answer in far too many cases is war toys! How does a gift that teaches destruction and death honor the birth of the Prince of Peace?

We are raising children who are being desensitized to the horrors of war and who seek to solve problems with guns and battle.

For younger children, consider giving playdough, simple musical instruments, puppets, dolls, Legos, art supplies, cassette tapes, trucks, puzzles, flashlights, magnets, fire engines, easels and paint, building blocks, and books.

For older children, think about magic kits, sports equipment, hobby kits, radios, cameras, fun clothing, lessons of any kind, models, board games, CDs, sleeping bags, wild jewelry, and books.

Of course the gift they want dearly is the gift of your time. One day as I was racing around the house, putting up the decorations and running off to a meeting, my son asked me to play a game with him. In my rush I said, "Can't you play with one of your toys?" But his response opened my eyes and my heart.

"But don't you know that no toy is gooder than a mother?" he said.

Plan the events for December to include the children. They don't want to spend the month with babysitters. Church and school festivities are important and provide good family time. Give up the office party and do something as a family. Go to the tuba Christmas concert or on a sleigh ride; volunteer to carol for shut-ins or open your home to someone or some family in need.

Traditions—without them our lives would be as shaky as a fiddler on the roof. Why do we do so much of what we do? Because of tradition. Traditions are wonderful, comfortable, and comforting. They can also become a checklist of obligations.

When I was a child my mother always baked cutout Christmas cookies and let all four of us do our own cookie decorating. She would make frosting in every hue, including the bright blue we loved even before the Cookie Monster. The entire kitchen was white with flour and the floor crunched with sugar and chocolate jimmies for days.

However, I've discovered that I hate being the mother part of this tradition. I can't cut out a decent cookie for love nor money. No matter how hard I try, I always cut the dough too thin (the only thin thing in my life!). My cookies always broke when we tried to frost them and I hate making dough. The whole tradition made me ill.

I stuck with it until I thought hard about what a tradition should do for you. This one did not give me a warm, happy feeling.

When I told this to a group of friends, they introduced me to a grandmother who loved to cut out cookies and didn't have any young grandchildren. She offered to be our Cookie Grandma and for the last five years she had made cookies and sent them over for the children to decorate. Now mind you, I don't mind the crunchy floor, it's just the baking process I abhor.

So we still have cookies, the kids still get to lick the frosting bowl, and we have a wonderful, dear new friend.

The last few years our boys have even volunteered to help her with the baking.

Not all traditions are dealt with that easily and happily. But since there is only one fruitcake in the world that is passed from family to family, I'm going to wait for my turn. We do cheat a bit and make our gingerbread house out of graham crackers and leftover Halloween candy. No, orange and black don't look terrific at Christmas, so I buy generic gum drops and lollipops. The children do the decorating and it's the last decoration I take down after the holiday. It truly is a work of love and creativity.

If a tradition is a burden, think it over, change it, alter it, or forget it. Children will take hold of a new tradition and guard it closely. You might have a special holiday breakfast, host a tree lighting party, light an Advent wreath each evening or fix a food basket for the hungry to teach the joy of giving.

It's time to take control of your holidays. Don't let them control you. And watch how the lights will sparkle as the true joy and meaning of Christmas return.

Mary Liebetrau resides in West Bend, Wisconsin.

A NEW HOLIDAY

My father's death at Christmastime nearly twelve years ago changed our holiday dinners forever. He was a patriarchal force at the head of the table and his death interrupted our family traditions.

Perhaps out of my own sense of "homelessness," I scouted through a rough neighborhood of our city distributing posters announcing that there would be food and coffee at a busy corner one Christmas Eve following my father's death. There we were, Mom and I and other helpers, handing out hot coffee and bag lunches when most families were home enjoying the evening as it was meant to be enjoyed.

Since that Christmas Eve we have found our way to new levels of celebrating and enjoying the season. And we have talked more about reaching out to the homeless with our simple gifts.

If your family is experiencing a loss during this joyful time of year, consider welcoming into your family those for whom loss is an everyday way of life.

Timothy Schultz resides in Atlantic City, New Jersey.

TRADITIONS TO PASS ON

THANKSGIVING EVE AT CHURCH

O n Thanksgiving Eve our pastor held a private family candlelight communion. One family at a time entered the candlelit sanctuary and had prayer, Bible reading, and communion. It was beautifully done. We were gracefully reminded that the Lord should be at the center of every celebration.

Lisa D. Hughes resides in Phoenix, Arizona.

HANDS ACROSS THE TABLE

American holidays are strongly laced with family togetherness. Having been foreign missionaries for most of our adult lives, and having no biological children, we have learned to find family wherever we are.

At present our lives are entwined with international students, helping them adjust to a new culture, learn English, and develop friendships with Americans, all for the ultimate purpose of sharing Jesus.

Since we are involved in an international conference over Thanksgiving weekend, we celebrate with out international "family" Wednesday evening, combining a dinner and Bible study.

Early arrivals like to migrate to the kitchen to watch the dissection of the turkey, many never having tasted it before. When most have arrived, song sheets are handed out, and after some explanation of words, we sing "Come, ye thankful people come."

Across the hall in a second apartment (part of which we sublet), candles are lit on the tables with festive place settings. The guests fill their plates from the buffet in the first apartment and fill the tables across the hall. There is an explanation about why turkey, corn and lima beans, cranberry salad, and pumpkin pie are traditional, amid many comments and laughter.

After dessert and coffee, more papers are passed out giving a brief history of Thanksgiving, appropriate Scriptures on giving thanks, songs, and then a chance for everyone to verbalize their own thanks. Usually *everyone* says something, even if in halting English. (We often have visiting parents of students.)

The evening ends with a wonderful sense of good will and comradeship.

Pete and Mim Stern reside in Philadelphia, Pennsylvania.

KERNELS OF THANKS

On each plate set on our Thanksgiving table are several kernels of corn. Before eating we take turns going around the table saying something we are thankful for, for each kernel of corn we have. As we say each thing, we drop a kernel in a basket on the table. It's a great way to review the year and be thankful even for things that happened a while ago, and also to share those blessings with family members.

Becky S. Shipp resides in Flint, Michigan.

ANGELS AND MORTALS

Sometimes memories serve to fuel the creation of other

TRADITIONS TO PASS ON

memories. I don't know if we were inspired by *It's a Wonderful Life* or just by the spirit of the season, but several years ago my home church created a game called "Angels and Mortals." Because some of my family's fondest memories have resulted from this game, we now play it each year.

Unlike most games, anyone who plays "Angels and Mortals" is a winner. The rules are simple: We put each one's name on a slip of paper and then place the names in a hat. Each person draws a name and becomes that person's "secret angel."

Over the course of the holiday season, each "angel" must secretly do nice things for his or her "mortal." At the end of the holidays we have a party and tell each other who our mortal was. In addition to being great fun, this game gives us a sense of just how thankful we should be for the unseen things real angels do for us each day.*

> *Twila Paris is an acclaimed singer and songwriter of Christian music.*

PEACE ON EARTH

The lion and lamb, symbol of peace, is the emblem of our church, so each year we try to find Christmas cards depicting a lion and lamb. Over the years we have amassed quite a collection with many unusual scenes. We always save a card to add to our Christmas treasures and each year we enjoy looking at the many varied scenes from jungle settings

---

From: Making A Christmas Memory *by Twila Paris with Jeanie Price. Copyright 1990. Used by permission of Tyndale House Publishers, Inc. All rights reserved.*

to snowy landscapes, yet all symbolic of "Peace on Earth."
Mickey and William Harris reside in
Escatawpa, Mississippi.

AN ADVENT SUPPER

The board of education at our church has for years sponsored a family soup and sandwich supper to precede the first Wednesday Advent church service. A craft hour follows the meal and then the church service starts at 7:00 P.M.

The craft project consists of something that would enhance our Advent season—a wreath, banner, decoration, and so on. Usually there is a family project to work on together and also easy projects that young children can accomplish alone. A small fee is charged for the meal and the craft to cover expenses.

Barbara Johnson resides in Eau Claire, Wisconsin.

AN OFFERING FOR JESUS

To remember whose birthday we are celebrating, we use a small gift-wrapped box that has a hole on the top. We set the box by our nativity scene on a shelf. For three to four weeks before Christmas members of our family drop spare change into the box as a gift to Jesus. The Sunday before Christmas our special offering is taken to church and given as a birthday present to Jesus.

Chris Brown resides in Jones, Michigan.

CUP OF CHEER

Each member of our family has a hot chocolate mug with

a brightly colored Christmas design on it. At the beginning of December we make hot chocolate, pour it into our mugs, add little marshmallows, and sprinkle colored sprinkles on top. We stir the delightful concoction with candy canes! This simple tradition, relished by our children, will be a memory that will last for a lifetime.

Judy Senne resides in Kansas City, Missouri.

FAMILY OF GOD

Visit morning and evening Sunday services of several different denominations. This may prove to be the best part of the holidays, as you are reminded that the family of God extends outside your own church and circle of friends. (Someone who is living alone or feeling lonesome might find this activity particularly satisfying. Why not invite them along?)*

THE FAMILY THAT READS TOGETHER

Set aside a time for family Bible reading every day in December, maybe right after breakfast or supper. You can make sure preschoolers don't feel left out by giving them a beautiful bookmark to mark the correct passage. Here are some daily suggestions:*

Nov. 30—Isaiah 42:1–9   Dec. 1—Psalm 89:1–29

*From: Great Christmas Ideas *by Alice Chapin. Copyright 1992. Used by permission of Tyndale House Publishers, Inc. All rights reserved.*

Dec. 2—Isaiah 55
Dec. 4—Luke 1:26–38
Dec. 6—John 1:11–18
Dec. 8—Malachi 3:1–4
Dec. 10—Mark 1:1–13
Dec. 12—Isaiah 52:1–6
Dec. 14—Luke 1:5–25
Dec. 16—Luke 1:39–56
Dec. 18—Luke 1:57–80
Dec. 20—Rev. 21:1–7
Dec. 22—Rev. 1:10–18.

Dec. 3—Isaiah 35
Dec. 5—John 1:1–10
Dec. 7—Micah 5:2
Dec. 9—Matthew 118:25
Dec. 11—Isaiah 40:1–11
Dec. 13—Isaiah 9:2–7
Dec. 15—Luke 2:8–20
Dec. 17—Jeremiah 33:7–16
Dec. 19—Isaiah 61
Dec. 21—Matthew 2:1–12

HOW TO WAIT FOR CHRISTMAS

"I can't wait 'til Christmas!" the children exclaim. It often seems a *long* time until Christmas comes, especially when store decorations go up right after Halloween. To help shorten the wait, in our house, we try to have "mini-celebrations" throughout December.

Early in the month we have a children's Christmas cookie decorating party for our two girls and their friends. We bake the cookies ahead of time, color canned frosting in several colors, and stock up on sprinkles. The children decorate one big cookie for their snack and one to take home. I read a Christmas story to them and then we play a few games like "Hunt for the Christmas Ornament," "Toss the Candy into the Muffin Tin," or "Pin the Nose on Rudolph."

Our girls, ages seven and ten, enjoy learning how people in other countries celebrate Christmas. We celebrate St. Nicholas Day on December 6 by putting small presents and Christmas candies in their dolls' shoes. They each get to open a present that day, a Christmas coloring or craft book, paper dolls, or a book.

On December 13, St. Lucia's Day, our oldest daughter dressed in a white nightgown with a red sash, wearing a cardboard and felt crown of candles that she had made. She served us cinnamon rolls, made the day before. We read parts of *Kirsten's Surprise* by Janet Shaw (Pleasant Company, 1986), a Swedish Christmas story. By having these fun times to look forward to, the long wait seemed shorter to them.

Janet M. Blair resides in Ansonia, Connecticut.

A STORY WITHOUT EQUAL

Preparations for Christmas used to start in our house about October, at least the most meaningful one I can remember after these sixty years.

At our daily evening devotional time, Daddy would have our family start memorizing the account of Christ's birth as recorded in Matthew or Luke, alternating one or the other each year. By the time Christmas arrived, we were able to quote the Scripture account by heart.

This was so meaningful to me as a child that my husband and I carried on that same tradition with our own five children. Our firstborn could recite Luke 2:1–20 when he was four years old.

Now we have twelve grandchildren, some of them teenagers. Last year two of our daughters and their families shared Christmas Day with us. At our traditional time for devotions, three generations rejoiced together at the incomparable Scripture account of Christ's coming as Savior, through the reciting of the various passages by memory.

Rachel O. Picazo resides in Morehead, Kentucky.

LETTERS TO MY SONS

At the holiday time I write a letter to each of my boys. In the letter I review things that have happened over the year, accomplishments that they have had, sometimes even their shoe size or batting average. I also tell them again how proud of them I am and how much I love them. I let them read the letter and then I put it away. I had originally thought I would give back the letters when they turned eighteen. I have decided, however, to continue the tradition until each one is out of college.

Diana M. White resides in Scotts Valley, California.

THE TEN DAYS OF CHRISTMAS

When our children were small, we started a tradition of the ten days of Christmas. My husband Tim and I would set up our nativity scene in a prominent spot. Then on the 14th of December (ten days before Christmas Eve), we would begin special devotions: Each devotion centered on a figure in the manger scene and always came back to the theme of Jesus' birth, God's special gift to us. Each child was allowed to hold the figure and pass it on to another. The figure of Baby Jesus would be last, with Tim emphasizing the celebration of Christ's birthday on the following day. Our children really enjoyed this for many seasons. If for some reason we forgot, they would remind us!

As the children reached their teen years, we were fortunate enough to go away for a family holiday at Christmas. About seven days before Christmas Day, we began our "special" devotions. This time we read from books like *How Silently, How Silently* (J. Bayley), *The Best Christmas*

Pageant Ever (B. Robinson), and *God Came Near* (M. Lucado). Then after discussion and prayer each person was allowed to take one item from their Christmas stocking. Stocking stuffers thus became an important "treat." Even though our family is grown, this sharing of stocking stuffers is still an important holiday time. We look forward to this expression of our love for each other and for Jesus, God's ultimate present to us all.

Sheila Hudson resides in Athens, Georgia.

CHRISTMAS CARD LONGEVITY

Beautiful (and expensive) Christmas cards have such a short life that I am always delighted to hear of people who have found ways to extend the pleasure they bring.

When I was a child, Mother invented games for us to play with the avalanche of cards that came to our house. We would tax our brains to learn the signatures then see who could do best at naming the sender just by looking at the front of the card. It became harder and harder as the pile grew larger.

Or, one child would pose as a figure from one of the cards, with everyone else trying to guess which one he had chosen to portray. No question about it—we enjoyed those cards for weeks. By the time we tired of them they were almost too worn to recycle in traditional ways.

Friends who have received my Christmas card poems tell me a variety of ways they have extended their life. One used hers as a Bible bookmark, another as a tree ornament, another as guest-room reading material.

All of my family look forward to the greetings sent each year by an artistically talented cousin. Painstakingly, with dainty lettering and intricate cutwork, she creates these cards, one by one. I'm sure we all cherish them, but one recipient does more. As Christmas approaches, she takes down her antique china from the plate rail in the dining room and displays the accumulated collection that now contains more than thirty beautiful works of art.

Among my acquaintances is a closet artist. Each year he selects the most beautiful card he has received that year and reproduces it in oils, in a size suitable for framing. Each Christmas season the regular pictures come down and his Christmas reproductions go up. Plagiarism? I think both the artist and the greeting card company would consider it an accolade.

Busy people sometimes don't give cards the attention they merit when they first arrive. One pastor's family saves the cards to savor one-a-day throughout the year, including the sender in their daily prayers. They do not concern themselves with selecting the most beautiful, nor creating a seasonal display, nor entertaining themselves with the cards. They concentrate on the sender.

Perhaps that response is the one most appropriate to the spirit of Christmas—that time when Love came to earth, to stay all year 'round.

Barbara Sutryn resides in Montoursville, Pennsylvania.

A TREE FARM OUTING

In our house everyone loves to participate when it is time to put up the Christmas tree. We've extended the excitement of that by going to a tree farm each year. There we walk through the vast selection of trees until we find the perfect one and Dad chops it down. After the tree has been put on the car, we warm up with hot chocolate, sometimes taking the hayride offered by the tree farm. Then, it's back home to trim our tree and enjoy some eggnog and Christmas cookies.

Christine Beckett resides in Matawan, New Jersey.

STARS IN YOUR EYES

On a clear night, bundle up in warm clothes and go outside to look at the stars. In the dark, talk about the star of Bethlehem and the coming of the Christ-child and His message of love. Go around the family circle and ask each to name one thing he remembers about Jesus' life and mission. See how many times you can go around the circle. Sit on a bench, blanket, or tarp and count stars.*

SLEEP UNDER A TREE

Let the kids sleep in sleeping bags under the Christmas tree the night after Christmas. It's fun to look up through the branches toward the top of the tree, and to fall asleep with the soft glow of the tree lights. For safety, an adult should be sure to turn the lights off after the youngsters are asleep.*

A SPECIAL CHRISTMAS GAME

As a mother of two daughters it was important to me to start a tradition when they were very young that would go

---

*From 101 Ideas for the Best-Ever Christmas. *Copyright 1992 by Caryl Waller Krueger. Excerpted by permission of the publisher, Abingdon Press.*

with them through the years. As we decorate the tree we choose ornaments that are special to us and hide them on the tree. Fraser fir trees are great because they allow you to tuck ornaments deep inside the tree. Thus begins our Special Christmas Game.

All the lights go out and we sit or lounge around the tree and try to find each other's ornaments! It's fun to search all over the tree for those special ornaments that mean so much to us. When the ornaments are found, one by one, a story is told about where each ornament came from and a very special Christmas memory is relived.

Toni Sims resides in Kosciusko, Mississippi.

CHRISTMAS READING

Since my husband and I have been married, we've made it a tradition to buy a new book each year that is focused on Christmas. Every December, we pull them all out and have a special time each day for reading and rereading them. There's a wide selection—children's, fiction, and so on—and we've enjoyed all of them.

Annette McEndarfer resides in Worcester, Massachusetts.

A NATIVITY TRADITION

When our son Jonathan was two years old, we received a lovely, hand-painted nativity set complete with people, stable animals, sheep, and camels. We would sit together as a family and read the Christmas story while moving the appropriate figurines into place. Each year Jonathan eagerly awaited the unpacking of the nativity set and we would again read the story of our Lord's birth and act it out with the figurines.

A few years later Brian was added to our family and I vividly remember the Christmas when he was two years old. When we unpacked the nativity set, Jonathan excitedly called out, "Brian come here, let me show you the story of baby Jesus!" As I watched, he told the story from memory and showed Brian what each piece was and the part it played in the story. He had some difficulty explaining the angel to a two year old who thought that anything with wings had to be a bird.

Day by day through each holiday season the nativity scene changes appearance as different family members arrange it while practicing the Christmas story. Those figurines now bear the evidence of being handled by young hands, but we don't treasure the nativity set for its physical beauty. Rather, we treasure it for what it has birthed in the hearts of our children and the precious gift from God that it represents.

Kelly Lutman resides in Lansing, Kansas.

THE MEANING OF THE ORNAMENTS

My German grandmother used to tell me tales of all the ornaments on the tree. When my own three sons were old enough to comprehend their meanings, I told them the beloved stories, and now my grandchildren are enjoying them as well.

The star on top of the tree symbolizes the star of Bethlehem that shone, leading the three wise men to the stable where Jesus lay.

The lights are all the other stars twinkling in the sky.

The garland wraps around the tree like a mother's arms

wrapped around her babe, loving and protecting it.

The round ornaments signify the earth that God created for man. The colors are different and each represents something special. Red is for Jesus' blood that was shed to redeem us. Blue is the for the skies that glow by sunlight during the day and shimmer by moonlight during the night. Green is for the trees and plants that God created to provide food for us. Silver and gold are for the rich blessings that He has given us.

The tinsel glistens like little sparks of fire, like the fire Joseph probably made to keep Mary and Jesus warm.

And the tree itself is full of life, adorned, standing proudly and pointing to heaven where Jesus waits for us . . .the tree seems to say, "Happy Birthday, Jesus, Happy Birthday!"

Janet Smith resides in Sunnyvale, California.

GOD'S GREATEST GIFT

Each Christmas, we set out our nativity set and leave the baby Jesus wrapped. On Christmas Day, we let our little one unwrap the baby Jesus as we talk about God's gift to us—His Son.

Charlene L. Cragg resides in Moreno Valley, California.

SAVE THAT DECORATING

It can take me two full days to decorate our Christmas tree and about four hours just to put on the lights. I'm particular. So you can understand why my sister said things would have to change when my son was born—no way would my tree ever be the same again.

When my son's first Christmas rolled around—he was eleven months, walking quite well, and into everything— I decorated my tree as usual from the top down to just about his eye level. I gathered up all his stuffed animals that were relatively small and decorated them with Christmas ribbons and wreaths and then purchased some small Christmas teddies and reindeer (about six inches high). This menagerie hung on the lower limbs of the tree and Daniel spent his days arranging and rearranging them.

When he got older and I could have my whole tree back, we purchased another tree for upstairs. We decorated it with the original menagerie plus all Daniel's other stuffed animals.

Today we decorate our family tree together and Daniel is a particular as I about how things are arranged.

Roxanna T. Sieber resides in Villisca, Iowa.

CHRISTMAS IN MIAMI

How do you celebrate Christmas in Miami when the weather outside is 84 degrees? I turn the air conditioner way down, put on a sweater, and play Christmas carols on high. For an Ohio-born girl dreaming of a White Christmas, it's the best I can do.

Of course, then we celebrate the real reason for the season—that God came down to earth! That's why we love to celebrate! That's why we decorate our homes. It's an act of gratitude and worship. For me the Christmas tree is the crowning touch. Scripture says "the trees of the field shall clap their hands," and I want our tree to sparkle as a standing ovation to our dear Savior, Jesus.

Last December we had a tree trimming party and invited some friends who had not participated in our tradition because of their Jewish faith. They seemed pleased to be a part of the family gathering as we feasted on a sumptuous buffet of wassail, roasted tenderloin, cheese grits soufflé, and countless goodies.

After dinner, we all got to work decorating. I had to smile at all the action. All ages and shapes were bending and stretching around the tree, placing each ornament in just the right spot. Several grandmothers, playing artist, painted freshly baked gingerbread boys, dipping their brushes in cups of tinted frosting. Throughout the evening, the most action centered around the tarts and cakes on the dessert table! With Christmas carols playing softly, it was a happy scene.

Then at last, with satisfied tummies and warm hearts, we basked in the glow of our work of art, the Christmas tree. In that shining moment, I prayed silently that my Jewish friends would know our love for them, and perhaps catch a glimpse of God's great salvation:

"For unto us a child is born, Unto us a son is given, And His name shall be called Wonderful Counselor, the Mighty God, the Everlasting Father, the Prince of Peace."*

Marabel Morgan is the author of
The Total Woman (*Revell*) *and other best-sellers.*
She resides in Miami, Florida.

---

*Taken from: Marabel Morgan, The Total Woman Cookbook, *Fleming H. Revell, a division of Baker Book House Company, Copyright 1980.*

KIDS' BAKING DAY

When our two children were about six and eight years old, we began a tradition rather accidentally. On the Saturday I planned to bake holiday cookies my children wanted to invite four neighborhood children over to help. I agreed (wondering where my sanity was), and soon I was overseeing six little people as they measured and stirred and mixed and licked. I've forgotten how many different kinds of cookies and candies we made that day, but I've never forgotten the fun it was. At one point I instructed my son Darrin to "stir it 'til the lumps are out." He looked at me so innocently and asked, "Can't I just eat the lumps out?"

Kids' Baking Day happened one Saturday every December until my daughter was a senior in high school. By then I had been retired from the kitchen and the kids had taken over the baking. Sure there was flour in places where flour doesn't belong and batter on the cupboard doors, but the laughter and good times will always be part of our memories. We look at the pictures in the family album and remember those wonderful Kids' Baking Days.

Judy Lovitt resides in Ogden, Utah.

CHRISTMAS IN THE 1920s AND 30s
As I Remember It

"They're going to build a toyland town all around the Christmas tree." Surely the composer of "Santa Claus Is Coming to Town" must have taken his inspiration from Baltimore in the 1920s and 30s. Everyone who could, had a "Christmas Garden" at the base of his Christmas tree. We were no different.

After Thanksgiving dinner was cleared away, we kids (my brother Wilson and I) were banished from the living room (and often the dining room) until Christmas morning. What interesting and curiosity-arousing sounds came from there! But we were never given a hint of what was going on.

You see, there was a friendly rivalry between my day and Mr. Baum who lived two houses down. They tried to outdo each other with their gardens. If we knew what was going on, we could have easily let it slip in a bragging session with Billy or Bobby Baum.

Although the theme changed from year to year, there was one constant—a model train that invariably derailed in the tunnel through the man-made mountains or on the far side of the garden (flush with the wall four feet away). We had an "O" gauge in the early days, but when Wilson was old enough he *made* from kits an "HO" set. (The only way you could get them was to make them.)

Wilson used matchsticks for the railroad ties and he also made his own houses and stations. Once he used plans published in *Better Homes and Gardens* to make a darling little house. That year he also made a factory and a station, all to the HO scale.

But back to Dad's garden. We had a fountain that ran spasmodically using recirculated water. That was always in the city square. But one year Dad added a waterfall and stream that ran the length of the garden (usually fifteen feet, the length of the living room). He drilled two holes in the living room floor to run pipes from the basement laundry tub and back again. (Wonder what the person who bought the house thought of those two holes in the living room floor!) Whenever anyone came to see the garden, one of us had to run downstairs to turn on the water to the shouts of "Too much! Little more! Hold it there!" That year Dad had outsmarted Mr. Baum for sure.

Another time that he thought he had outsmarted him was the year of the amusement park. But Mr. Baum had come up with the same idea. Of course, Wilson and I thought ours was the best by far. And, of course, the Baum boys thought theirs was best.

I don't remember details from theirs, but ours had a playground with swings that swung, seesaws that see-sawed and a merry-go-round that twirled, all with tiny, tiny dolls on them. I was "allowed" to dress the dolls although I didn't know what they were for until Christmas morning.

There were other moving things but I can't remember what they were. Except the roller coaster! (In Baltimore this was known as a "racer dip.") Dad had gotten thin strips of wood to build it from leftovers from my uncle's cigar box factory. I can remember Wilson bringing them home on the streetcar.

A little car with more of the dolls in it climbed the long ascent to the top of the roller coaster, and took off from there! And I mean took off! One time it went sailing across the living room. (Dad never could figure how to slow that thing down, and along with it the swing, seesaw, and so on that sent dolls into space until he thought to glue them to their seats.)

One time the preacher came to "see the garden." After a demonstration of the marvels of our amusement park, he took an envelope out of his pocket and wrote on it, *"Ride at Your Own Risk!"* and stuck it on the side of the roller coaster.

One year we had a moving roadway that carried little cars along. That became a source of great amusement when someone set the rheostat too fast.

In those days homes weren't decorated. People would put their trees near a window so that the lights could be seen at night. Several blocks down the street next to us there was a row of homes with sun parlors (windowed rooms attached to the front of the houses). The people who lived there would all put their trees in the sun parlor. We would take a walk on Christmas night just to see those lighted trees. To my young mind they were thousands of jewels sparkling in the night.

Those who lived in the city would put their gardens next to the window because the sidewalks came right up to the house. They would enjoy watching folks as they walked up to the window to see the garden. Often, seeing people looking in, they would start the train running. (Almost everyone had a train.) One of our week-after-Christmas activities was to ride around town on the street-car and see all the trees in people's houses.

But not only private homes had Christmas gardens. Most of the fire stations also had them. The firefighters would park one or more of the engines outside the station (sometimes starting in the summer) and spend their spare time creating lavish gardens. In the 1950s and 60s one engine house had the four seasons depicted. For winter they had skiers going down a slope (they had learned how to control the speed) and in the summer section they had a drive-in movie using a small screen TV. Another station had a harbor scene with a ferryboat going back and forth and other ships coming and going. Usually you had to wait your turn to see these creations from the firefighters.

Much later when I married, our first Christmas "tree" was a branch cut off my mother's large tree and stuck in a jar of water. Our "garden" consisted of some houses cut from cereal boxes and set at the base of the "tree" on the game table. As the years rolled by and the children came, we had more traditional gardens, but nothing could compare with the ones of my childhood.

Margaret L. Matthews resides in Columbia,
South Carolina.

AFTER THE KIDS GO TO BED

This is a simple holiday idea that is so obvious and yet for some reason my husband and I didn't take time to do this for years. After we put the children to bed, we turn off the television, put on some Christmas music, and turn off the other room lights. We sit and enjoy a warm drink, watch the pretty Christmas tree lights, and talk.

Kimberly Miller Wentworth resides in Colbert, Georgia.

A TIME TO ENJOY

Each Christmas season we begin giving our gifts about a week before Christmas. When the children were young and received a lot of gifts we began this tradition by giving one gift each day starting about one week before Christmas. Even now as teenagers our children so look forward to receiving these gifts and are able to take time to enjoy them more. On Christmas day there is not a mad rush to open gifts—and not enjoy them.

Donna M. Hoult resides in Philadelphia, Pennsylvania.

THE PLAY'S THE THING!

When our children were small we always met at my sister's house on Christmas Eve. Grandparents on both sides were there too. One Christmas the children were so excited they were distracting us as we did last-minute preparations for the meal. I suggested they go downstairs and prepare to act out the nativity scene for us after supper, before we opened gifts.

Not only did they do a great job that year, but it became a family tradition. As they got older they even wrote their own stories and acted them out as plays. This tradition is spreading to the next generation as we are now the grandparents.

Mildred S. Barton resides in Anderson, South Carolina.

THE JOURNEY TO BETHLEHEM

Make a wall map of Joseph and Mary's journey from Nazareth to Bethlehem showing the route they may have taken: villages along the way; rivers, lakes, and mountains; and estimated number of miles between places. Children can even clip pictures from magazines or Christmas greeting cards to depict the scene more graphically. If the family enjoys this project, continue with a map showing the flight to Egypt. Read the Bible accounts to get as much information as you can for accuracy.*

---

*From: Great Christmas Ideas *by Alice Chapin. Copyright 1992. Used by permission of Tyndale House Publishers, Inc. All rights reserved.*

A SUNRISE PICNIC

Establish an annual sunrise picnic some weekend morning during the holiday season. Take along bacon, eggs, potatoes, an old frying pan, a coffee percolator you don't care about, and plastic dishes and utensils. The kids can gather twigs and sticks to build a fire while adults peel potatoes, prepare the coffee, and set the table. After breakfast there will be woods and pleasant trails to investigate and beautiful bird songs and squirrel and chipmunk antics to enjoy.*

COME HOME FOR CHRISTMAS

Coming home for Christmas will cost much more for larger families, but holiday separations mean there is a vacuum in the heart, a small sad feeling that will not go away because someone is missing. One suggestion is for all families to covenant together to put away twenty dollars a week (or per month) for a holiday reunion the next year. If there's an accountant in the family, perhaps the money each month could be sent to him or her to be put in an interest-bearing account. If the plan works, and everyone wants to try it again, family members can take turns hosting so nobody has the burden over and over.*

A SERVICE AT HOME

For years the entire family would attend Christmas Eve services at our church. However, as grandchildren began to arrive, at least one adult would not be able to share in the service in order to stay home with the children.

Since 1966 we have held our own Christmas Eve candle lighting service. The service begins with Grandpa Clarence offering prayer and reading those passages from the Bible telling of the birth of Christ. Each person's candle is then lit, and we all join in singing "Happy Birthday, Jesus," followed by Christmas carols. A sumptuous meal follows.

Clarence Blasier is the compiler of The Golden Treasury of Bible Wisdom (*Barbour Publishing, Inc.*).

JUST WAIT UNTIL DARK!

On Christmas Eve my husband and I and our two children wait just until dark and then we pile in the car and drive all over town to see our favorite lights. Afterward, at home, we have homemade oyster stew and crackers and hot cocoa or spice tea. When we're finished, we light candles, turn off the lights, and sing (individually or all together) our favorite Christmas carols and hymns *while recording ourselves*. We are sometimes serious and sometimes silly. Then one of us reads the birth of Christ from the Bible and we pray. The children are then allowed to open one gift before going to bed.

Tracey Nobles resides in Casper, Wyoming.

MAKE MERRY MUSIC

Music has always been a part of Christmas at the Donaldsons'. As a youngster I enjoyed listening to the cousins join together to create a mini-concert for my grandparents. My father, aunt, and grandmother took turns at the piano and my mother and uncle would read a poem or short story.

Years have passed but the tradition has carried on. The younger generation now does all the planning and work as they share their God-given talents. The "Donaldson 5" plus spouses join their voices in singing favorite Christmas carols and my father plays his favorite hymns on the organ. There are many surprises as well as new music combinations that are tried. An attempt at a flute, saxophone, and french horn trio and a guitar duet of "Jingle Bells" have been, needless to say, entertaining.

Thank You, God, for the talents You have given our family. Most of all, thank You for Your Son Jesus. He is the reason we celebrate and carry on the tradition.

Bethel Donaldson resides in Ogema, Wisconsin.

A STORY TO REMEMBER

I wanted my children to anticipate the holidays while they remember the real reason for the season. Last fall we memorized one verse each week of Luke, chapter 2. When the holidays arrived my four year old and two year old could recite the Christmas story straight from God's Word! As they recited Luke's account at each family gathering, Christ became the focus for all of us. The children's self-esteem was boosted as both felt such a sense of accomplishment.

Kay Fuller resides in Forest City, Iowa.

A SOUTH TEXAS CHRISTMAS

In our family we get together on the Friday night before Christmas. Previously we have drawn names and bought a gift for one person only. We gather at my house for the gift exchange and food. We enjoy a traditional South Texas feast of hot tamales, pinto beans, chips and dips, and sweets. At this gathering we take hundreds of photos. We have made many memories over the years and the photos bring back precious loved ones no longer with us and how we all looked "back then." We also keep a guest book each year and everyone signs in, even the little ones!

Zula Shenk resides in Robstown, Texas.

CHRISTMAS EVE POTLUCK

We all meet after church on Christmas Eve and share a potluck dinner. After earing and visiting we have our most meaningful event of the evening. Each family shares something that is on their hearts. For example, one family does a silly skit, one sings, one shares some Scripture verses. My father always shares the story of Christ's birth and then he talks a little to the grandchildren about keeping Christ first during these hard years. After all the presentations we sing "Happy Birthday" to Jesus and have a piece of His birthday cake. The children then exchange gifts. With such a big family—six children, all married, and eleven grandchildren—we are thankful we can all be together to have such a great time in Jesus.

Sharon E. Jacobson resides in Hitchcock, Texas.

A CHRISTMAS PRAYER

To help our young children develop a spirit of thankfulness, each night during the month of December we have a special time of prayer. We begin our time by turning off the lights and lighting several candles. We stand in a circle holding hands (or a child) and thank the Father for several things and then for His Son. We blow out the candles and the children then go to bed with good, loving thoughts.

EVANGELISTIC CHRISTMAS PARTY

Every year we host or assist in an evangelistic Christmas party. What better time of the year to gather children together and share with them the true message of the holiday! The party includes games, songs, a Bible story (a presentation of the Gospel), and a lot of fun. We have seen many children come to believe in the Lord Jesus as a result. Child Evangelism Fellowship is an excellent resource for such an endeavor.

Annette McEndarfer resides in Worcester, Massachusetts.

FIRST ONE UP!

Since our children were small we have tried to focus on Jesus' birth and the true meaning of Christmas. Here's a tradition we began a few years ago. The first person who wakes up on Christmas morning—before he or she even gets out of bed—yells out loud, "Happy Birthday, Jesus!" Through the years it's always interesting to see who will be the first one to wake up. I don't think it's ever been

Dad or Mom! The first year we did this I was surprised to hear my youngest who was four yell out bright and clear. She beat her two older brothers!

Jill Bomberger resides in Salem, Ohio.

A FUN FAMILY GIFT EXCHANGE

Last Christmas I couldn't afford to purchase any lavish gifts for my family, so I decided to put the emphasis on fun instead of money. I bought many small but useful inexpensive items, such as a calendar, boxes of stationery, a photo album, and so on. I didn't put name tags on any of the wrapped gifts. Each person chose a gift, one at a time, and opened it. The next person could then choose whether or not to take that gift or pick a different one from the pile. When something you like is taken from you, and you have to choose a new gift all over again, you have to laugh about it.

Lisa D. Hughes resides in Phoenix, Arizona.

THESE THREE GIFTS

Because Jesus received gold, frankincense, and myrrh, our children each receive three gifts on Christmas morning. Gifts include something they want (usually a toy), something they need (usually an outfit), and something fun and educational (the parents' choice).

The children's gift lists are well thought out and short, and as parents, we keep from overindulging our children. We have never heard "Is this all there is?" on Christmas morning. Most importantly, all of us keep our focus on Jesus.

Anne Brophy resides in Troy, Michigan.

OPEN BY THE NUMBER

We have solved the problem of rattling packages and knowing the gift before it's opened. Every year all the gifts to the children have numbers on them, but no names. Mom has a hidden list of what name goes with what number. On Christmas morning the children (right now there are seven still at home) take turns calling off numbers and Mom looks on her list and lets them know who gets what number. . .but no one opens! When all gifts are passed out and stacked in front of each child, Mom tells who should open what number. There is no more paper flying as one gift is opened at a time. Mom even gets to see gifts being opened (as does everyone else) and thank yous get said. After ten years, no one has found Mom's special list!

Sheila Truhlar resides in Manhattan, Illinois.

THE PROPER FOCUS

To keep the focus of Christmas on the birth of Jesus, we have always kept the "under the tree" gifts in a separate room of the house. We let our preschooler play with the ornaments on the tree and role-play with the manger scene under the tree. Of course, many of the ornaments end up more on the floor than on the once carefully decorated tree! We bring in the gifts on Christmas Day when we are ready to open them.

Sharon Cofran Skinner resides in
Pembroke, New Hampshire.

A TRADITION OF SONG

In my family, we conclude our Christmas dinner by singing "The Twelve Days of Christmas." Each dinner guest finds their "part" when they sit down as each table setting as a "day of Christmas" glass by it. We have had some wonderful moments as our "choir" sings. Each year we make an audiotape of the song and now—years later—it is nice to sit back and listen to our collection and "feel" those voices that no longer grace our earth, yet come home again at Christmas.

Ann Davies resides in Valparaiso, Indiana.

TAKE TWO CRANBERRIES

Before Christmas dinner, put two fresh cranberries on each plate. After the family is seated, pass around a basket and, as cranberries are dropped in, share two ways in which Christmas is special to us. Follow by reading John 3:16, and conclude with prayer.*

---

*Let's Make a Memory, *Gloria Gaither and Shirley Dobson, Copyright 1983, Word, Inc., Dallas, Texas. Used by permission.*

AN UNDECORATING PARTY

For years I took down the tree after Christmas all by myself and would feel kind of sad about it. One year my husband suggested we make a party of it and now I look forward to it. We put on Christmas music and I make hot chocolate and popcorn. We drink, eat, and talk as we take the ornaments off the tree. When it is all finished we go out to eat at a favorite restaurant.

Kimberly Miller Wentworth resides in Colbert, Georgia.

DO-IT-YOURSELF NEW YEAR'S EVE PARTY

Everyone brings a covered dish!

As each guest arrives, they draw a slip assigning them a specific duty:

Pour Beverage
Pass Snacks
Clear Dishes
Load Dishwasher
Etc., Etc. . .

Now the *Fun* Part!!! Crazy Hat Contest!!!

Host couple provides the following: One old newspaper per couple. Scotch tape, paper clips, staple gun, ribbons, wrapping paper (left over from Christmas), plus colorful items such as old silk flowers and feathers. Place all material in center of room and allow thirty minutes for everyone to create a millinery masterpiece!

Award prizes for as many categories as you wish:

- Silliest
- Most original
- I wouldn't be caught dead in this!
- Most aerodynamic
- Most ecologically sensitive

And, of course, everyone cleans up their own mess before accepting award.

> *Hermine and Al Hartley are the author-illustrator team that created the best-selling book* The Family Book of Manners (*Barbour Publishing, Inc.*).

LET IT SNOW!

Our family enjoys going sledding and roasting hot dogs and marshmallows on New Year's Day.

> *Glenda Kreiman resides in Lindsay, Montana.*

Festive Beginnings

SHRIMP DIP

One 8-oz. package
  cream cheese
1 cup chopped shrimp
  (boiled)
1/2 tsp. Worcestershire sauce

1/4 tsp. garlic
1/2 cup mayonnaise
1/4 tsp. celery salt
1 bunch green onions,
  chopped

Let the cream cheese stand at room temperature until soft.
Mix all of the above ingredients together. Serve with crackers, or whatever you prefer.

Linda Duhan resides in Lafayette, Louisiana.

QUICK ONION DIP

1 pint sour cream
Chopped mushrooms
Chopped green or black olives
1 1/4-ounce packaged dehydrated onion soup mix
4 T. finely chopped English walnuts (optional)
Chopped pimientos

Blend together sour cream (or imitation) and dehydrated
onion-soup mix. Add pimientos, green or black olives, or
mushrooms, according to taste. All should be well drained
before adding to dip. For variety, add English walnuts.
Keeps well up to one week in refrigerator. Store covered.

Taken from: The June Masters Bacher Country
Cookbook *by June Masters Bacher. Copyright 1988 by
Harvest House Publishers, Eugene, Oregon 97402. Used
by permission.*

GUACAMOLE

4 ripe avocados (peeled, seeded, chopped)	1/2 cup mayonnaise
3 T. lime or lemon juice	1/4 cup dry onion (peeled, chopped)
1 tsp. garlic powder (or 1 clove, chopped)	1/2 tsp. Tabasco sauce
	2 medium tomatos (peeled, diced)

2 tsp. chili powder and 1 tsp. salt, blended

Mash avocados with fork or purée in blender. Mix remaining ingredients except tomatos. May be prepared a day in advance. In order to retain color, push at least one avocado seed into dip and cover bowl tightly with plastic wrap. When ready to serve, remove avocado seed, garnish dip with tomatos, and sprinkle with paprika.

Taken from: The June Masters Bacher Country Cookbook *by June Masters Bacher. Copyright 1988 by Harvest House Publishers, Eugene, Oregon 97402. Used by permission.*

BEAN DIP SUPREME

1 can (16 ozs.) refried beans	4 oz. green chilies
4 oz. taco sauce or salsa	4 oz. sour cream
1 1/2 cups shredded Cheddar or Monterey jack cheese	
3 oz. black olives	Tortilla Chips

Chop green chilies and black olives. Spread refried beans across bottom of shallow 9-inch ovenproof dish. Follow with a layer of chilies and a layer of taco sauce. Cover with cheese. Bake at 350°F until bubbly (about 20 minutes).

Top with black olives and dollops of sour cream. Serve with tortilla chips.

Therese Hoehlein Cerbie resides in
Harrington Park, New Jersey.

FRESH SALSA

5 ripe tomatos   1 bunch scallions
1 T. whole coriander seeds
2 small cans green chopped chilies
1 T. each: hot water, salt, sugar, red wine vinegar,
  olive oil
Tabasco sauce or Louisiana hot sauce to taste.

Crush whole coriander seeds and add hot water. Let sit. Chop tomatos and scallions, including tops. Add green chilies and mix. Add sugar, salt, vinegar, and olive oil. Add drained hot water "juice" from coriander seeds to salsa mixture. Add Tabasco to taste, about 5 to 10 shakes. Makes enough for 2 bags of tortilla chips!

Ellen Caughey resides in Harrington Park, New Jersey.

CHEESE STRAWS

2 cups all-purpose flour   2/3 cup butter
Dash of red pepper   3 T. cold water
1 3/4 cups sharp cheese, grated

Cut butter into flour with pastry cutter. Stir in cheese and pepper. Sprinkle with water. Stir with fork and work into dough. Roll out on floured board. Cut into narrow strips with fluted pastry wheel, about 3 inches long. Bake at 350°F for about 10 minutes. Makes about 150. Sprinkle with grated Parmesan cheese before baking. Place carefully in a box with waxed paper between each layer and give as gifts.

June Blackford resides in Nicholasville, KY.

CHRISTMAS CHICKEN LOG HORS D'OEUVRES

Two small cans of chicken	8 oz. cream cheese
1/3 cup diced celery	1/4 cup chopped parsley
2 tsp. A-1 Steak Sauce	1 tsp. curry powder

Mix together and refrigerate 4 to 12 hours. Just before serving take the chicken out and roll it into a log shape. Mix a cup of chopped walnuts and a cup of chopped parsley together on a cookie sheet and roll the log in the mixture so that parsley and nuts cover the outside. Serve on a plate with small crackers all around. Provide a knife so people can serve themselves bite-size portions on bite-size crackers.

Stormie Omartian is a best-selling author, singer, and fitness expert. Her books include A Step in the Right Direction (*Thomas Nelson*) *and her autobiography,* Stormie (*Harvest House Publishers*).

AUTHENTIC ENGLISH WASSAIL

Spiced oranges:
Stud 3 oranges with whole cloves, 1/2 inch apart. Place in baking pan with a little water and bake slowly for 30 minutes at 325°F.

Wassail:

3 quarts apple cider	1/2 tsp. nutmeg
1/2 cup honey	1/3 cup lemon juice
2 tsp. lemon rind	5 cups pineapple juice
Two 3-inch cinnamon sticks	

Heat cider and cinnamon sticks in a large saucepan. Bring to boil. Simmer, covered, 5 minutes. Add remaining ingredients and simmer, uncovered, 5 minutes longer. Pour into punch bowl and float spiced oranges on top, using cinnamon sticks for stirring or put into crockpot on high to keep hot. Makes 40 cups.

Kathleen Yapp is a versatile and prolific writer who resides in Gainesville, Georgia. Among her inspirational romances is Golden Dreams *(Heartsong Presents).*

MERRY SALADS

CLARA'S BEST CRANBERRY SALAD

1 lb. fresh cranberries	Rind of one orange, grated
1 small can crushed pineapple	1 1/2 cups sugar
1 cup crushed pecans (optional)	1 large box any kind of red gelatin
1 cup boiling water	1 package plain gelatin
1/2 cup cold water	1 large pkg. cream cheese

Dissolve the red gelatin in boiling water. Dissolve the plain gelatin in 1/2 cup cold water. Put in blender or food processor. Add fresh cranberries until well crushed. Add the cream cheese and sugar. Pour into a large bowl and add all other ingredients. Let chill and serve. Serves eight people easily.

Linda Herring is a first grade teacher as well as a published writer of inspirational romance. Among her books is Dreams Fulfilled *(Heartsong Presents). She resides in Monahans, Texas.*

COLLEEN'S TASTES-LIKE-MORE POTATO SALAD

4 medium potatoes
  (cooked and cooled to handling temperature)
  (best to use White Rose potatoes)
1 medium onion, chopped fine
  (better yet, several green onions with tops),
4 hard-boiled eggs, cooled and chopped
4 dill pickles, chopped fine

Toss lightly with a prestirred blend of mayonnaise, prepared mustard, and a little dill pickle juice and pepper. Good served right away or chilled. Either use right away or put in refrigerator until needed.

Variations: Black or ripe olives, cherry tomatos, and/or fresh parsley can be used for garnish.

Colleen L Reece is one of the most beloved writers of Christian romance. She resides in Auburn, Washington.

CHRISTMAS FRUIT SALAD

This fruit salad was a favorite in the Morris household, so when I married a Morris forty-four years ago, I had to carry on this tradition.

2 large cans fruit cocktail	4 or 5 bananas, sliced
1 cup pecans, chopped	2 T. Miracle Whip

Mix fruit cocktail, bananas, and pecans together. Chill in refrigerator overnight. Add Miracle Whip the next day and mix in well. Serves 8 to 10. This makes a good dessert with white cake.

Johnnie Morris is married to Gilbert Morris, best-selling Christian author (with Bobby Funderburk) of A Call to Honor *and* The Color of the Star *(Word Publishers). The Morrises reside in Baton Rouge, Louisiana.*

CRANBERRY RELISH

I like to make Cranberry Relish at Thanksgiving and then freeze half of the relish for the busy Christmas season.

4 medium oranges, seeded	2 pounds cranberries
4 medium unpeeled apples (cored)	4 cups sugar

Take the yellow peel from oranges; trim off and discard white part. Put orange pulp and yellow peel, cranberries, and apples through food chopper. Add sugar and mix well. Makes 4 pints.

Irene Burkholder resides in Leola, Pennsylvania.

FAVORITE HOLIDAY FRUIT SALAD

1 can peach pie filling
1 no. 2 can pineapple tidbits (drained)
One 11-oz. can mandarin orange slices (drained)
I box frozen strawberries (thawed and drained)

Mix above at last minute, cut 1 large banana, pour 1/2 cup lemon juice over it, and drain. Add to above and chill. *Optional*: 1/2 cup blueberries or 1 can drained fruit cocktail can be added.

Bessie R. Fortenberry resides in Brandon, Mississippi.

CRANBERRY JELLO

6-oz. package cherry gelatin (1 large or 2 small packages)
2 cups boiling water
1 can whole cranberry sauce
1 16-oz. container sour cream
1/4 cup chopped walnuts

Mix gelatin with boiling water; stir until dissolved. Stir in
canned cranberries and pour into wreath-shaped mold.
Chill until thickened (about 1 hour). Stir in sour cream and
nuts. Chill until firm. Remove from mold and serve.
Holiday Note: For Christmas, empty a box of green gelatin
into small mixing bowl and prepare according to direc-
tions on box. When firm take a knife and slide along side
of bowl and ease into center of cranberry gelatin wreath.
Top with whipped cream if desired.

JoAnn Otto resides in Cortland, New York.

HEARTY ENTREES

ROAST BEEF TENDERLOIN

One 6-pound whole beef tenderloin
1 clove garlic   Kitchen Bouquet
Freshly ground pepper

About 1 1/4 hours before serving, preheat oven to 450°F.
Remove any surface fat and connective tissue from tenderloin. Rub surface with garlic and Kitchen Bouquet. Press
fresh pepper in meat.

Place on wire rack in shallow open pan, tucking narrow end under to make roast more uniformly thick. Insert
meat thermometer into center at thickest part. Roast about
60 minutes or until thermometer reads 140°F. Meat is
crusty brown outside, pink to red inside.

Cut tenderloin into 1-inch-thick slices; arrange on
heated platter. Spoon BÉARNAISE SAUCE over slices or
serve it from gravy boat. Makes 8 to 10 servings.

BÉARNAISE SAUCE

3 shallots or little green onions, chopped fine
1 tsp. dried tarragon   1/4 cup wine vinegar
1/4 cup white vinegar   1 T. lemon juice
1/2 cup butter, softened   1/2 tsp. salt
Dash of Tabasco sauce   2 tsp. chopped parsley
3 egg yolks

Bring to boil in saucepan shallots, tarragon, and both

vinegars. Boil until sauce become glaze. In heavy saucepan, mix egg yolks and lemon juice with wire whisk.
Over low heat or hot water, beat in butter, 1 T. at a time,
until thickened. Stir in glaze and rest of ingredients. Serve
warm with roast beef.*

> *Marabel Morgan is the author of*
> The Total Woman (*Revell*) *and other best-sellers.*
> *She resides in Miami, Florida.*

CHRISTMAS BEEF BARBECUE

One 3-pound roast beef, baked tender
1 bottle (regular size) catsup
2 shakes Tabasco sauce
Horseradish per individual taste (optional)

After beef roast has cooled, shred apart in a large bowl. In
a small bowl mix catsup, horseradish, and Tabasco sauce.
Combine catsup mixture with meat and cover until ready
to use. When ready, warm mixture and serve on large buns.

> *Margaret Layton Hunt resides in*
> *Charlotte, North Carolina.*

CABBAGE ROLLS

1/2 lb. hamburger	1/2 cup ham (cut fine)
(uncooked)	1 small onion
1 cup rice	Salt and pepper to taste

Taken from: Marabel Morgan, The Total Woman Cookbook, *Fleming H. Revell, a division of Baker Book House
Company, Copyright 1980.*

Mix all together. Roll in cabbage leaves and place in baking dish. Add some water and bake in 375°F oven until rice is tender (approximately 1 hour). (If you put cabbage in boiling salted water and boil about 2 minutes and drain the leave, they can be pulled apart easily.)

Alice Schenk resides in Rupert, Idaho.

FESTIVE WAIKIKI MEATBALLS

1 1/2 lbs. ground beef	2/3 cup cracker crumbs
1/2 cup red onion	1 egg
(coarsely chopped)	1 1/2 tsp. salt
1/4 tsp. ginger	1/4 cup milk
1/2 tsp. garlic salt	3/4 cup red pepper,
3/4 cup green bell pepper,	chopped
chopped	1/2 cup shredded coconut
2 cups water	2 T. cornstarch
3/4 cup brown sugar	1 can pineapple chunks
1/2 cup vinegar	(13 oz. can—save juice)
4 T. soy sauce	1 sm. pkg. slivered almonds
1 small can water chestnuts (drained)	

Mix beef, crumbs, onion, egg, salt, ginger, milk, and garlic salt and shape into balls. Brown in skillet, pour off fat.

Mix water, brown sugar, juice from pineapple, vinegar, and soy sauce and bring to a rapid boil. Add cornstarch and mix until thickened (stirring constantly). Pour over meatballs that have been placed in baking dish or dutch oven. Place peppers, pineapple, coconut, almonds, and chestnuts around meatballs and bake at 300°F for 45 minutes or in a slow cooker on low for several hours.

Can be served on toothpicks as finger foods or over rice for a delicious meal.

Judy Boen resides in Bakersfield, California.

KRAUT BEROK

1 medium head cabbage	Salt and pepper to taste
3 large onions	2 pounds hamburger

Fry hamburger in large skillet until it begins to brown. Add chopped onions and cabbage. Add salt and pepper to taste and fry until cabbage is done.

Alice Schenk resides in Rupert, Idaho.

AFTER-THE-HOLIDAYS SPECIAL

2 cups diced turkey	1 cup celery
1/4 cup dry roasted peanuts	(sliced diagonally)
2/3 cup mayonnaise	2 T. lime juice
1/2 tsp. curry powder	1 cup pineapple chunks
1/2 cup sliced green onion	(drained)
1 cup seedless green grapes	2 T. chopped chutney
1/2 tsp. grated lime rind	1/4 tsp. salt

Toss together the first six ingredients. Combine remaining ingredients to make a dressing. Stir dressing into turkey mixture. Serve on a bed of greens. May be doubled or tripled.

Taken from The June Masters Bacher Country Cookbook *by June Masters Bacher. Copyright 1988 by Harvest House Publishers, Eugene, Oregon 97402. Used by permission.*

Sweet Endings

CANDY CANE COOKIES

This recipe is my personal favorite because of the decorative design it adds to a plate of cookies and also because I enjoy the taste of a soft brownie with peppermint icing.

Combine 3/8 cup hot water with 1 package dry devil's food cake mix. Mixture will be lumpy. If necessary, add drops of water very sparingly.

Roll into narrow logs about 8 inches long, curving one end to form the shape of a candy cane. Bake 8 to 10 minutes at 350°F on a greased cookie sheet.

When cooled, frost cookies in white: 3 cups sifted confectioner's sugar, 3 tablespoons hot water, 9 drops peppermint. Use red cake icing in a tube to add stripes.

Michelle C. Hooks resides in Apopka, Florida..

SUGAR COOKIES

Creating Christmas cookies has been a tradition in the Civitts family. As grandchildren come and go, with flour on their faces and delicious dough in and out of their mouths, this special time has molded and shaped their lives, making us a stronger family. The following recipe only gets better as the years go by.

2 cups sugar	2 eggs
1 cup shortening	1 cup milk
1 tsp. baking soda dissolved in 1 T. of water	

Mix the above ingredients and add:
  3 tsp. baking powder   Pinch of salt
  Nutmeg or lemon

Add flour (about 2 sifters full) until thick and pour on floured table. Knead. Refrigerate.

While dough is still cold, use desired cookie cutters (some handed down for generations!) dipped in flour to prevent sticking. Bake at 350 °F. Frost and decorate when cooled.

Frosting

Mix together the following:
  4x powdered sugar (3/4 bag)   2 T. margarine
  3 T. shortening   3 egg whites
  Vanilla (or any flavor)
          Julie S. Long Civitts resides in Toccoa, Georgia.

MINUTE-MADE MACAROONS

  One 1-pound package shredded coconut
  One 15-ounce can sweetened condensed milk
  2 tsp. vanilla

Blend coconut into milk. Add vanilla and drop by tea-spoon onto well-greased cookie sheet. Bake 10 minutes (or until crusted but not brown) at 350°F. Cool 2 minutes before lifting individually with spatula.

Taken from The June Masters Bacher Country Cookbook *by June Masters Bacher. Copyright 1988 by Harvest House Publishers, Eugene, Oregon 97402. Used by permission.*

CRANBERRY-RAISIN PIE

1 1/2 cups sugar	1/4 cup orange juice
1/4 tsp. salt	Water
3 cups cranberries	1 cup seeded raisins
1 T. cornstarch	1 tsp. grated orange rind
2 T. butter	

Make pastry for two-crust 9-inch pie. Bring first 3 ingredients and 2 tablespoons water to boil in saucepan, stirring until sugar is dissolved. Add cranberries and cook, stirring occasionally until berries pop open. Add raisins. Blend cornstarch and 2 tablespoons water. Add to berry mixture and cook until thickened, stirring. Remove from heat and stir in fruit rind and butter. Pour into bottom crust. Add 2 tablespoons butter and cover with top crust. Bake 25 minutes at 425°F. Serve hot or cold. Good with whipped cream or a scoop of frozen vanilla yogurt.

> *Irene B. Brand is a well-known writer of inspirational romance. Among her titles is* Afterglow (*Heartsong Presents*).

CHRISTMAS PLUM PUDDING

1/2 cup apple, chopped	1/2 cup suet, chopped
1/2 cup molasses	2 eggs, beaten together
1/2 cup milk	2 cups sifted flour
1/4 cup figs, chopped	1/2 cup currants
1/4 cup candied cherries, (quartered)	1/2 cup raisins
	1/4 cup citron, sliced
1 T. orange peel, chopped	2 tsp. baking powder
1/2 tsp. each salt, baking soda, cinnamon, and nutmeg	

Combine apple, suet, molasses, eggs, and milk. Sift flour, measure, and mix 1/2 cup with dried fruit and nuts. Combine remaining flour with baking powder, salt, baking soda, cinnamon, and nutmeg. Add to apple mixture. Add floured fruits and nuts. Turn into decorative greased molds, filling 2/3 full. Cover and steam 3 hours. Cool. Wrap. Freeze until ready to use.

Serve cold with hot hard sauce, whipped cream, or flambé at the table. Use your favorite mixture for flambé or simply dip sugar cubes in lemon extract and light. In any case, surround with holly and sprigs of mistletoe.

Taken from The June Masters Bacher Country Cookbook *by June Masters Bacher. Copyright 1988 by Harvest House Publishers, Eugene, Oregon 97402. Used by permission.*

ICE CREAM YULE LOG

Our family traditionally indulges in this dessert after Christmas dinner.

3 pints quality ice cream (cylindrical containers)
Cherries and mint leaves (for decoration)

1 pint chocolate ice cream
1/2 cup sliced almonds
Mocha fudge sauce (below)

Set a long platter in the freezer to chill for at least 30 minutes.

Slide a knife around the insides of the ice cream, then ease the ice cream out onto the chilled platter. Push ends together to form a log and smooth the joints with a spatula.

Freeze until firm, at least 15 minutes.

Soften the chocolate ice cream until it is the consistency of thick frosting. Working quickly, spread chocolate ice cream over the frozen log on the platter. Freeze until firm.

Garnish log with almonds, mint leaves, and half cherries. Slice and top with fudge sauce to serve.

Mocha Fudge Sauce

1 1/2 cups semisweet chocolate chips
3/4 cup whipping cream   3 T. strong coffee

Stir chocolate chips and whipping cream together over low heat until just melted. Stir in coffee. Serve warm. (This may be made ahead and refrigerated for up to a week.)

Sara Everett resides in Hesperia, California.